Bright Ideas
Christmas Activities

Written by Mary Smart

Contents

Published by Scholastic Publications Ltd,
Marlborough House, Holly Walk,
Leamington Spa, Warwickshire CV32 4LS.

© 1987 Scholastic Publications Ltd
Reprinted 1988, 1989
Some ideas drawn from Scholastic
magazines.

Written by Mary Smart
Edited by Jackie Cunningham-Craig
Sub-edited by Jane Hammond
Illustrations by Chris Saunderson

Printed in Great Britain by
Loxley Brothers Ltd, Sheffield

ISBN 0 590 7083 1

Front and back cover: designed by Dave Cox,
photograph by Martyn Chillmaid

Introduction

The weeks before Christmas are always very busy – decorations, presents and productions are all in full swing – and sometimes teachers might worry that many areas of the curriculum are neglected.

This need not be the case; integrated learning can continue with one or two aspects of Christmas as the focus of activity. The children's work can then be displayed to produce a cheerful and seasonal atmosphere in school.

Christmas offers a wide and varied range of activities. Interesting legends and customs going back over many hundreds of years give insights into how people used to live; different parts of the world have developed a variety of celebrations often with a common thread – a good opportunity to think about the celebrations and festivals of other cultures.

Language, mathematics, science, cooking and problem-solving, as well as art and craft, can be included.

Christmas Activities emphasises children as active learners, making decisions and choices whilst working at their own level. Appropriate ages and group sizes are given for each section, but this will vary from individual to individual and from group to group.

Whatever the age, children enjoy doing as much as they can for themselves so, if an adult is doing the work rather than supporting it, the task is too difficult and should be adapted if possible.

Some of the activities are based on working as individuals, but there are also plenty of opportunities for children to co-operate in groups.

Whatever they do, I hope that the children and you will enjoy it!

Mary Smart

Christmas around the world

Merry . . .
No one's hangin' stockin's up
No one's bakin' pie
No one's lookin' up to see
A new star in the sky.
No one's talkin' brotherhood
No one's givin' gifts
And no one loves a Christmas tree
On March the twenty fifth.

Shel Silverstein (from *Where the Sidewalk Ends*,
copyright Jonathan Cape)

Celebrations are held all over the world at around the time we call Christmas. Customs and rituals often have their roots well into pre-Christian times but have been adapted to become part of Christmas activity.

Different countries have developed versions of the same legends – for example, Father Christmas or Santa Claus appears variously around the world as St Nicholas (Holland and Belgium), Père Nöel (France), the Christkindl Angel (Germany and Austria), Julenisse elves (Denmark), Baboushka (Russia) and Befana, the Good Witch (Italy). All bring gifts to children and most involve them in little traditions and rituals.

During the Middle Ages in Germany, St Nicholas took on the role of present giver. He was the Bishop of Myra in Turkey and died in AD 345 or 352. He is said to have heard of three young sisters unable to marry because their father was too poor to afford a dowry. St Nicholas wanted to give the money anonymously and, in one version of the story, he threw purses filled with gold in through the girls' window on three successive nights. In another, he dropped them down the chimney and they fell into the girls' stockings which were drying by the fire.

These days, in Holland, St Nicholas arrives on 6 December having travelled from Spain by sleigh. He has gifts for all the children who have been good but his assistant, Black Peter, has only pieces of coal for those who have been naughty.

In Germany, the Christkindl Angel looks for children's present lists which are left propped up by the windows. She rings a bell and leaves presents.

Find out how to write Merry Christmas in as many different languages as possible (photocopy pages 95 and 96); an imaginative display of these could help children understand the international significance of cultural festivals.

Have you been good?

Age range
Any who can write.

Group size
Individuals.

What you need
Photocopy pages 98 and 99, pencils, pens.

What to do
Children could write a justification for being on the 'good' list but they might also make a separate list of the not-so-nice things they have done. They could be asked to share one thing from each list for a class discussion.

Present lists

Age range
Any who can write.

Group size
Individuals.

What you need
Sugar-paper, paints including gold and silver if possible, chalk, scissors, writing paper, gold and silver pencil crayons, photocopy page 97.

Doll
Bicycle
Trainers
Puppy
Dress
Roller boots
Necklace

What to do
Get the children to draw the outline of a life-sized angel using chalk. They should then cut out the outline and paint it on *both* sides.

Ask them to write out a list of presents (using a copy of page 97) leaving a margin all the way round to illustrate with angels and presents. Paint the drawings in gold and silver. Then ask them to write a second list of presents to give to other people and illustrate in the same way. Stick the lists on each side of the angel and display it on a window.

Denmark

In Denmark Santa Claus is helped by small elves called the Julenisse. They carry a lantern to work by and if children don't leave them something to eat they can get quite hungry and grumpy!

Julenisse elves

Age range
Five upwards with some help.

Group size
Individuals.

What you need
Thin card or stiff paper, art straws, PVA glue, scraps of material and brightly-coloured paper, paints and crayons.

What to do
The children should cut the the card or paper into a circle with a 15cm radius. Fold the circle in half and cut into two semicircles. Shape and stick one semicircle into a cone and snip off the point (see figure 1).

Figure 1

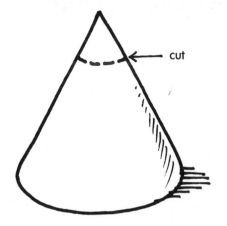

cut

Pleat a piece of white paper, fold over and twist the ends together (see figure 2).

Figure 2

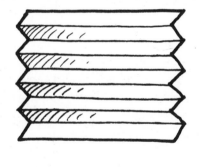 

Put the twisted ends into the top of the cone to form the elf's head. Secure by sticking or stapling. They can paint the face in whatever colour they think an elf's face might be and leave to dry. Make two armholes in the cone and thread through an art straw. Dress the elf in scraps of material, draping over the straws for sleeves if required. Use felt-tipped pens or paints to add features to the face; stick on hair and make a hat out of coloured paper.

Clay Julenisse

Age range
Six upwards.

Group size
Four or five children.

What you need
Clay, clayboard, tools.

What to do
The children should mould a solid cylinder of clay with a diameter of about 7 or 8 cm and between 15 and 20 cm long. About 6 cm down gently squeeze to form the head. Just below the head flatten the body to make shoulders, torso and legs (see figure 1). Use a clay tool to cut a gap

Figure 1

Figure 2

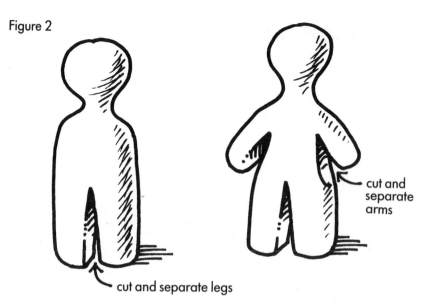

cut and separate arms

cut and separate legs

to make the legs and arms (see figure 2).

Make sure upright models have a broad enough base to stand steadily. Hats can be made by shaping a cone of clay from a semicircle and carefully adding it to the head (see figure 3). Details to the face and clothes can be made with clay tools. After biscuit firing, the elves can be glazed in opaque white, adding detail with oxides.

Figure 3

Julenisse 'snacks'

Age range
Five upwards.

Group size
Individuals.

What you need
Paper, 'snacks' with price tags
or photocopy pages 100
and 101, toy money,
felt-tipped pens and pens.

What to do
What sort of things do the class think elves would like to
eat to help them through their busy night? Provide them
with some 'snacks' with price tags and let everyone have
a set amount of 'money' to make a selection. Get them to
make a 'plate' from a circle of white paper and list their
choices in the middle. Draw a picture of these choices
and colour in felt-tipped pens all round the edges.
Alternatively, get them to fill in copies of pages 100
and 101.

What can the children find out about Danish food? Is
their traditional Christmas dinner like ours? What sort of
Christmas treats do they have?

Heart decorations

Age range
Ten upwards.

Group size
Individuals.

What you need
A rectangle of gold
paper 15cm × 20cm,
a rectangle of
silver of the same size,
scissors, glue.

What to do
Christmas tree decorations in Denmark are traditionally
home-made hearts. The class will enjoy making these.
Place the rectangles on top of each other, metallic side
up, with the long edge of the rectangle across the top (see
figure 1). Fold the two together and draw one side of the
heart. Cut it out (see figure 2).

Figure 1

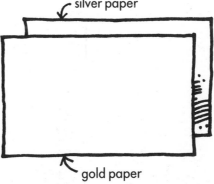

Figure 2

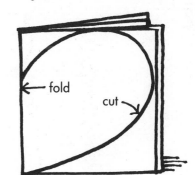

Open it out. With the two hearts still together, cut three diagonal lines across them and cut the top left-hand part of the hearts right away (see figure 3).

Figure 3

cut away

Separate the pieces of paper and turn them to look like figure 4.

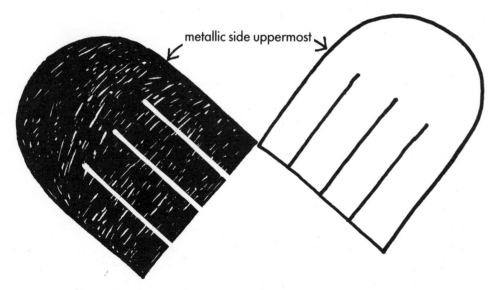

metallic side uppermost

Figure 4

Weave them together. Glue ends down and trim the edges (see figure 5).

Figure 5

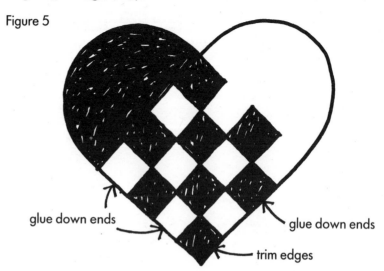

glue down ends

glue down ends

trim edges

Add a loop to the cleft of the heart and hang it from the Christmas tree. Other good colour combinations are red and green; black and gold; blue and silver, and red and gold.

Italy and Spain

Italian children are visited by Befana – a beautiful, smiling witch who climbs down chimneys to put presents in the shoes of good children; the not-so-good are supposed to get charcoal. Befana was a house-proud woman who entertained the three kings on their way to visit Jesus, so her gifts are distributed at Epiphany, 6 January. Spanish children leave their shoes on the balcony at this time so that the kings can fill them with presents as they pass.

A life-sized Befana

Age range
Five upwards
with some help.

Group size
Five or six children.

What you need
2 pairs of children's tights,
newspaper, thread,
bodkin,
about 25 cm of stockinette,
wool, old clothes,
material off-cuts.

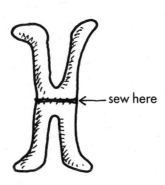

What to do
Get the children to soften the newspaper by crumpling it into balls and stuff both pairs of tights. They should be quite firm. Sew the two waists together (see figure 1).

Figure 1

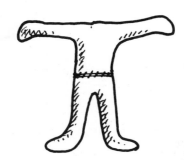

← sew here

Move the legs of the top pair of tights into the arms position (see figure 2).

Figure 2

Tie one end of the stockinette together, stuff it with softened newspaper and tie the top. This is the head. Sew it into place.

Decide what sort of clothes a magical – and good – witch might wear and 'dress' her. The dressing-up box might prove a useful resource here. Paint her face either directly or as a mask. Add tumbling curls – unravelled knitting or curled strips of paper. Sit her astride a broomstick and suspend her from the ceiling.

Shoes to leave for presents

Age range
Eight upwards.

Group size
Individuals.

What you need
Clay, clay tools etc.

What to do
Get the children to look at their shoes carefully – how do they fasten? What shape are they? Feel the space their feet go in and make a drawing of it.

Give each child a piece of clay to make into a three-dimensional oval shape (a spheroid), using their thumb to make the space inside it for the foot. Use tools to make the fastenings – holes for laces, buckles etc. Lengths of clay rolled between fingers make ideal laces! They should look carefully at the way the heel is arranged and reproduce it on their models. Make seamlines and patterns with the tools. Leave the model to dry out well before firing. Glaze in appropriate colours.

Russia

In Russia it is Baboushka, who offered food and shelter to the wise men on their journey to Bethlehem, who delivers presents to children. Like Befana she did not accompany them because she felt she should tidy her house first and when she finally arrived, Jesus had left! She is supposedly still seeking the Christ-child and at Christmas when she sees a sleeping child and hears of good deeds, she leaves a toy from her basket, just in case, then carries on with her journey.

Papier mâché Russian dolls

Age range
Seven upwards.

Group size
Two or three children.

What you need
Balloons or sand-filled polythene bags for moulds,
sharp knife,
thin strip of card,
pale emulsion paint,
felt-tipped pens,
varnish or PVA glue.

What to do
Tell the children to prepare moulds as shown in figure 1. Cover with several layers of newspaper and glue, ending with a layer of white kitchen paper. Use a pair of pointed

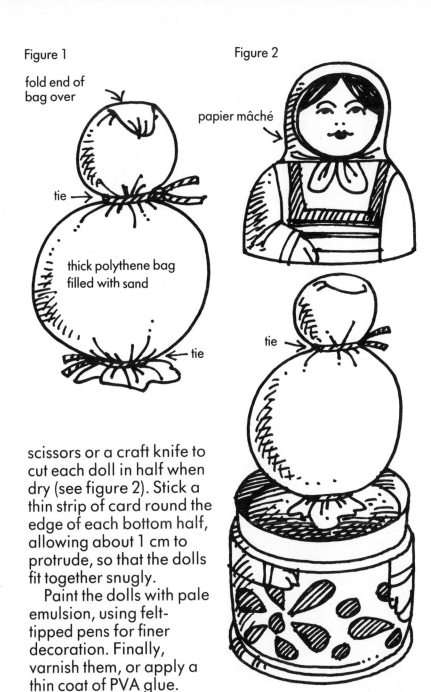

Figure 1

fold end of bag over

tie

thick polythene bag filled with sand

tie

Figure 2

papier mâché

tie

tie

scissors or a craft knife to cut each doll in half when dry (see figure 2). Stick a thin strip of card round the edge of each bottom half, allowing about 1 cm to protrude, so that the dolls fit together snugly.

Paint the dolls with pale emulsion, using felt-tipped pens for finer decoration. Finally, varnish them, or apply a thin coat of PVA glue.

Mexico

In Mexico children receive their gifts in a piñata – a brightly decorated clay pot, filled with tiny presents and sweets. It is hung up, just out of reach, and then broken by children who scramble for the presents as they fall from the broken pot. It might be a bit frustrating to spend a long time making and decorating a pot only to break it, so here is a version of the piñata which can be kept.

A piñata

Age range
Five upwards with some help.

Group size
About four or five children.

What you need
1 cup salt, 1 cup flour, cooking oil, aluminium foil, varnish, PVA glue, sweets, thread or ribbon.

What to do
Each group should mix the salt and flour with a little water to make a dough. Knead it until it is fairly smooth and mould it into two thumb pots. Put a ball of aluminium foil in the centre of each one. Place, curved side uppermost, on an oiled baking sheet and harden off in a low oven for about 40 minutes. (Make sure that children are supervised.) Remove the foil and decorate each pot with brightly painted designs; when quite dry they can be varnished or covered in PVA glue. Put a few sweets in one side, place the other on top and tie up with bright ribbon or thread. When they are hung up the sweets can be removed by children knocking them gently apart.

Norway, Sweden and Finland

Candles play an important part at Christmas-time in Norway, Sweden and Finland. They can be seen in the crown of St Lucia. The youngest daughter in each family is dressed as St Lucia and wakes her family with coffee and biscuits. These head-dresses are also worn during the Festival of Lights procession to celebrate Christmas.

Candle head-dress

Age range
Six upwards with some help.

Group size
Individuals.

What you need
Thin card,
gold and red
metallic paper,
scraps of gold
and red tinsel,
PVA glue, stapler
(optional).

What to do
Help the children to cut a strip of card about 6 cm deep and long enough to fit around the head. Cover this in gold metallic paper, making sure all the corners are stuck well down. For the candles, cut four more rectangles of card 4 cm × 11 cm and cover in the red metallic paper. To make the 'flames', cut an appropriate shape from card, cover with gold and stick a smaller piece of red inside. Add a scrap of tinsel for the wick (see figure 1).

Figure 1

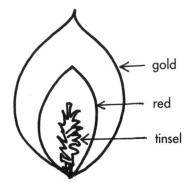

gold

red

tinsel

Assemble this together using PVA or staples. If using a stapler, make sure the open side of the staples is on the outside to prevent the wearer from getting scratched. Fit on to the head and fasten (see figure 2).

Figure 2

For more work on candles and light, see pages 48–57.

Poland and Hungary

Poland and Hungary remember King Wenceslas at Christmas, who was king of a country we know now as Czechoslovakia and, legend has it, was a compassionate man. The carol, 'Good King Wenceslas', recalls one of his generous deeds when he helped a peasant.

King Wenceslas' castle

Age range
Any age.

Group size
Any size – everyone could help with it.

What you need
A collection of cylinders of various sizes, stiff paper or thin card, silver paint, white paint, blue paint or metallic paper in the same colour, sheets of thin polythene, 'angel hair', glitter or glitter gel, PVA glue.

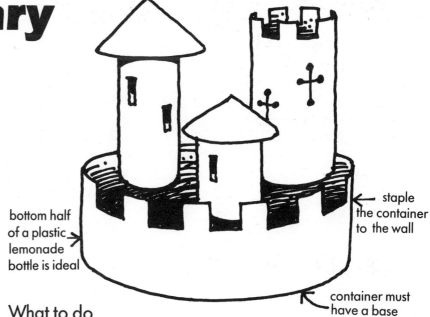

bottom half of a plastic lemonade bottle is ideal

staple the container to the wall

container must have a base

What to do
Ask the class or group to paint the cylinders using silver, white and blue paint or cover with metallic paper. Make cones as turrets for some, 'castellate' others. Use the glitter to simulate caps of snow on some of the cones. Paint some strips of card or stiff paper for castle walls, castellating the top.

Prepare a snowy background – white paint applied with sponges or white material is ideal. Staple a drum covered in paper to the background. Put some of the cylinders in a drum which has been painted or covered in paper. Continue to put the castle together using the strips of card as connecting walls – curve these outwards to give a three-dimensional effect. To create a misty and magical illusion hang the polythene in small pleats and folds in front of the castle. Drape the 'angel hair' around for more frost and mist. The children could make King Wenceslas and his page using the same cone technique as the Julenisse elves (see page 9).

Father Christmas

'Twas the night before Christmas, when all through the
    house
Not a creature was stirring, not even a mouse;
The stockings were hung by the chimney with care;
In hopes that St Nicholas soon would be there . . .

So begins one of the most famous poems about St Nicholas, written by Dr Clement Clarke Moore in 1822 for his own children. It may be the first complete description we have of the figure who is known to us as Santa Claus or, more usually, Father Christmas.

St Nicholas probably became known as Santa Claus because the Dutch words for St Nicholas – Sante Klaas or Sinter Claes – became Anglicised.

His image has changed somewhat over the years. Dr Clarke described him as a sort of short, round elf, who smoked a pipe. His picture first appeared in 1863, when Thomas Nast published a drawing in *Harper's Illustrated Weekly*, along with details about Santa's life, such as his home at the North Pole where he managed toy-making workshops throughout the year.

Nowadays we think of Father Christmas as a tall, rather imposing figure, still with the white beard but

without the pipe. It may be that the European Santa figure merged with an ancient pagan character from old English mummers' plays, Old Christmas, who has a beard, a humped back, a club in his hand and a wreath of holly on his head. He may have acquired a long red robe and replaced the club with the more festive sack of toys. This modern image was apparently inspired by a Coca-Cola advertisement from 1931 drawn by Haddon Sundblom.

However Santa evolved, he is probably the most powerful symbol of Christmas for children. But because the stereotype is so definite it is difficult for us to help children to develop their own ideas; it is too tempting to concentrate on the result rather than the process. But this can be turned to advantage, since most children can clearly articulate Santa's attributes which are simple enough to transfer to paint, paper and collage.

Father Christmas portrait

Age range
Five upwards.

Group size
Individuals – but small children will need opportunity for discussion.

What you need
Large sheet of sugar-paper, chalk, paints, scraps of black shiny material, white fluffy material, oil pastels, white glue.

What to do
Ask the children to draw the outline of Father Christmas in chalk first, making sure that the head is right at the top and the feet right at the bottom of the paper. Paint the main blocks of colour and leave it to dry. (Small children should use paint straight away.)

Use the selection of materials to add details, and the oil pastels to provide features on the face. (Younger children may find strong wax crayons easier to control for this.)

Rubbings

Age range
Seven upwards.

Group size
Any size.

What you need
Thin card, white glue, scissors, white paper, wax crayons.

What to do
Ask the children to draw a Father Christmas figure on a piece of thin card. Explain that, as they will be cutting out the rubbing, the arms and legs should not be too thin. Stick on additional pieces of card for the hat, beard and fur trim to make the relief. Finer details, such as facial features, belt, buckle, etc, can be added with drops of PVA glue. Allow this to dry really hard and then place a piece of white paper over the card shape. Rub with the broad side of a wax crayon, cut out the rubbing and mount it on contrasting paper for cards and calendars.

Papier mâché Santa

Age range
Six upwards.

Group size
Small groups.

What you need
1 fibre egg-box,
1 teaspoon of cold-water paste
(without fungicide),
1 teaspoon of Polyfilla,
paints,
varnish.

What to do
Tear the egg-box into very small pieces, put the pieces in a bowl and cover them with hot water. Leave them to soak for 48 hours, stirring occasionally. Drain off the water but don't squeeze the cardboard. Sprinkle on the paste and work the mixture until it is evenly distributed. Allow this to stand for 15 minutes, then add the Polyfilla and knead the mixture again. It will be lumpy but it is less bother than conventional papier mâché. Use the mixture to form a rounded cone shape for the body and a sphere for the head. Allow these to dry out thoroughly, then paint and varnish them, adding any other appropriate detail.

Letters to Santa

Age range
Six upwards.

Group size
Everyone can contribute.

What you need
Large piece of backing paper for the sky,
empty cereal boxes,
paint, sponge,
drawing paper,
crayons, photocopy
page 102.

What to do
Everyone writes letters at this time of year, so make them into a focus for display.

Using large pieces of sponge get the children to print the paper for the sky. Provide a variety of suitable colours – black, purple, dark blue, grey, etc.

Each child can then make a chimney by covering a cereal box with drawing paper and printing brick shapes on it, using either a cardboard cuboid or sponge. Father Christmases should be drawn and coloured, then fitted inside each chimney, with their letters stuck on the outside. Assemble the chimneys and other parts of houses produced in a similar way on the backing paper.

Encourage the children to think about the needs of other people by writing to Father Christmas about suitable presents for the less fortunate.

Christmas feelings

Age range
Eight upwards.

Group size
Whole class.

What you need
Michael Rosen's 'Has Father Christmas Forgotten Me?'

What to do
Everyone remembers what the night before Christmas felt like as a small child; older children will recall clearly the previous Christmas or even Christmases when they were very small. Read Michael Rosen's poem 'Has Father Christmas Forgotten Me?' to the class, and ask them to write a list of ten of their own feelings.

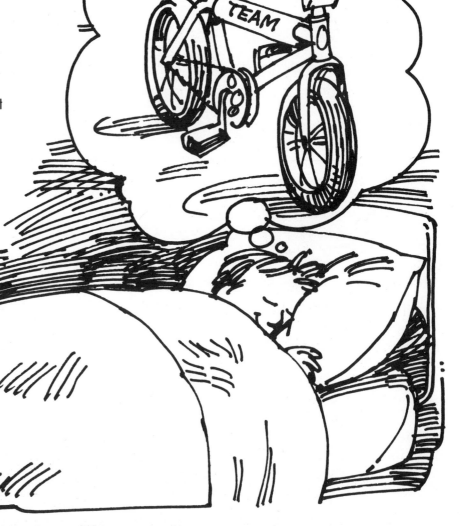

Has Father Christmas Forgotten Me?

It was Christmas Eve.
I knew Father Christmas
was mum and dad.
I knew he didn't come down the chimney
and instead
they came through the door.
I knew it didn't all come out of a sack
but instead
they left a heap of stuff at the end of the bed.
I knew it, I knew it, I knew it.
What I didn't know was what was going to be
    in the heap
But I went to sleep
so then I woke up.
Nothing.
So I went to sleep
so then I woke up.
Nothing —
was that piece of paper there before?
Must have been.
So I went to sleep
so then I woke up.
Nothing — except for that bit of paper.
So I went to sleep
so then I woke up.

Nothing —
and it's morning.
Has Father Christmas
    forgotten me?
I mean, mum and dad.
Get up.
Feeling bad.
Feeling worse than bad.
Terrible.
Nearly crying.
The piece of paper —
what is it?
It's a picture of a bike
and underneath it, it says:
DOWNSTAIRS.
so it's rush-rush downstairs,
front room,
and there it was,
propped up against a chair
in front of the telly.
Big and shining.
Of course,
Father Christmas couldn't stuff a bike
down the chimney, could he?

Michael Rosen

Wobbly Father Christmas

Age range
Seven upwards.

Group size
About six children.

What you need
For each Father Christmas:
half a ping-pong ball,
Plasticine,
2 dead matchsticks,
card.

What to do
Wobbly people are fun to make and provide a good starting point for an early understanding of balance and the force of gravity.

Ask the children to draw and cut out their Father Christmas and stick a matchstick at the bottom of each leg. Put the Plasticine into the halved ping-pong ball and then press the figure into the Plasticine, matchsticks first.

If they want the figure to wobble from side to side when lightly pushed but fall right over when pushed hard, how much Plasticine will be needed? How wide or tall should the figure be to make it work best? How many times does it wobble before it stops?

Flying reindeer

Age range
Seven upwards.

Group size
Small groups.

What you need
Empty washing-up
liquid bottle,
wire,
card,
Plasticine,
crayons,
paints.

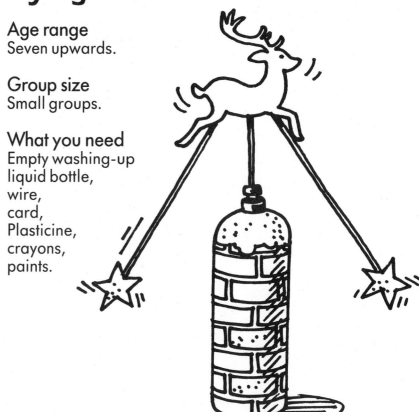

What to do
Get the groups to draw, cut out and paint a reindeer (see template on page 103) and two stars. Paint bricks on the washing-up liquid bottle, leaving a space at the top to represent snow.

A lot of discussion will be needed to decide on the length of the wires, the weight of the Plasticine blobs and the stability of the container before assembling this simple balancing toy.

Children will discover how to make it work by experimenting with making the toy balance.

Help Santa deliver the presents

Age range
Seven upwards.

Group size
Small groups of four or five.

What you need
A large sheet of card, felt-tipped pens, smaller pieces of card photocopy pages 104 and 105.

What to do
You can make this game for the children to play, or older children could plan one for themselves and each other.

Photocopy page 104 or draw a plan of three or four streets on a large sheet of card, name each street, draw the houses and number them. Make a 'stocking' of toys for each house and write the address of where it is to be delivered on the back (page 105). Cut the stockings out and put them in a box. The players have to devise an efficient way of sorting the stockings for fast and accurate delivery.

Reindeer stories

Age range
Five upwards.

Group size
Whole class.

What you need
Books, poems and songs about reindeer (eg 'Reindeer Report' – see below).

What to do
Father Christmas would not be complete, of course, without his reindeer. What would it be like to be a reindeer? Make a collection of stories, poems and songs written from this point of view. Then ask the children to write some Christmas reindeer stories, and make them into a book with appropriate illustrations.

Reindeer Report
Chimneys: colder
Flightpaths: busier
Driver: Christmas (F)
Still baffled by post-codes

Children: more
And stay up later
Presents: heavier
Pay: frozen

Mission in spite
Of all this
Accomplished
      U A Fanthorpe

Christmas cards

The only cards that really count
Are that extremely small amount
From real friends who keep in touch
And are not rich but love us much.

John Betjeman (from *Advent 1955*)

Cards play a very important part at Christmas but, of course, they are also sent at other times as well.

Get the class to make a list of all the occasions when they might send a card: eg birthdays; to wish good luck; congratulations for particular events; to wish people better health; at Easter; New Year, etc.

Ask the children to collect as many of these 'occasion' cards as they can and talk about who they might send them to.

A useful appreciation of cultures other than Christian might start from a collection of cards celebrating their festivals. They often depict important religious symbols: eg the Jewish Hannukah card may show the Menorah, the eight-headed candlestick, or a Muslim card may have a piece of the Koran in Islamic calligraphy.

You might want to go on to celebrate other festivals in your classroom such as the Hindu Diwali or Muslim Id, but before doing so, remember to check with parents and community leaders to avoid errors.

Symbols on cards epitomise Christmas and powerfully reinforce attitudes and perceptions. Cards with mother-tongue messages can help reflect this cultural diversity – as can the images around the classroom.

The first Christmas card was made in 1843 although its designer, Henry Cole, had trouble in persuading people that it wasn't just a frivolous waste of money. A thousand copies were made, costing one shilling each which is about the equivalent of £20.40 today (based on the Post Office's calculation that the penny post of 1840 would now be at least £1.70).

However, in less than 30 years, Christmas cards became very popular.

Cheaper printing processes from Germany created a big Christmas card industry in which thousands of people, including children, were employed. Some children had the dangerous job of keeping the machines clean whilst they were still in action.

These old Christmas cards are now very valuable. Some have been hand-painted by children because it was cheaper to use them for this work. One of Henry Cole's first cards would now fetch over £400.

Older children could make a study of child labour – chimney sweep boys, match girls, miners, etc – and find out what Christmas might have meant for them and other poverty-stricken people. Are there people today who don't have a good time at Christmas?

Printing cards

Many simple printing processes are possible in school for use with all ages. Discuss with the class the printing processes and then let them try their hand at one of the following methods.

Printing processes

Age range
Six upwards.

Group size
Whole class or small groups.

What you need
History and information on printing.

What to do
Look at the different methods of making prints with your class. If possible, visit a local printing press or newspaper office. Encourage discussion and project work.

Potato printing

Age range
Five upwards.

Group size
Six to eight children.

What you need
Potatoes, newspaper, pieces of thin sponge, thickened paint, coloured sugar-paper, black sugar-paper, craft knife, glitter, felt-tipped pens.

What to do
Each child needs half a potato on which to carve out a design. Young children will need to have this done for them. A Christmas tree, a bauble or a holly leaf are good shapes to begin with. Soak the sponge with the paint and use it as a printing pad. Encourage the children to practise on newspaper first and then make their design on the coloured sugar-paper. It could be embellished with glitter or additional details made with felt-tipped pens, etc. Mount the finished design on the black sugar-paper to make a card.

Matchstick prints

Age range
Six upwards.

Group size
Small groups.

What you need
Small strips of balsa wood or matchsticks mounted on to strips of card for easier handling, light green sugar-paper, thick dark green paint, white paint, scraps of sponge.

What to do
With a wet sponge and fairly dry white paint get the groups of children to print a background on the green

fold

sponge printing

sugar-paper. Let it dry. Meanwhile, they can practise printing with strips of wood. They could design a Christmas tree or spiky greenery or whatever appeals. These can be arranged on the white sponged background to make the card.

Fingerprinted cards

Age range
Six upwards.

Group size
Five to ten children.

What you need
Strip of thin sponge for a printing pad, thickened paint, sugar-paper.

What to do
Get the children to practise making fingerprint designs until they do one that they like – they can be as simple or as complicated as they want. Put the design on the sugar-paper and make it into a card.

fingerprint balloons

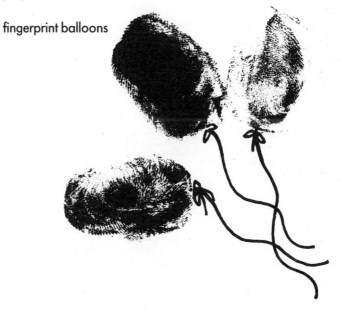

Polystyrene printing

Age range
Seven upwards.

Group size
Small groups.

What you need
Polystyrene food trays
or Plasticine,
string or card,
water-based printing inks,
rollers, thin paper.

What to do
The blocks for printing (see figure 1) can be made from
the bottom of polystyrene food trays or Plasticine, where
the design is incised by drawing into the surface or
pressing objects into it, or by raising up the surface for
printing using string or pieces of card.

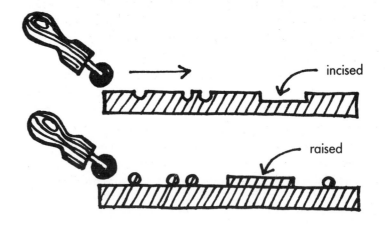

Before you start, ensure that the blocks and the paper
are the same size, making allowances for trimming and
mounting. All printing from polystyrene, Plasticine, string
or card blocks is best done using water-based printing
inks, rollers and thin paper. Prepare the children for the
inevitable production line rejects, and encourage them to
experiment with bold and simple designs and the
effective use of colour (see figure 2).

Figure 1

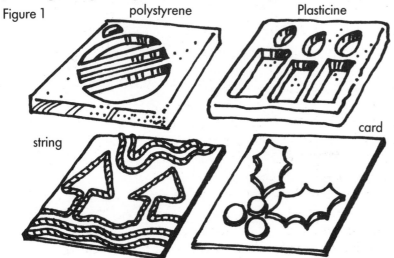

Figure 2

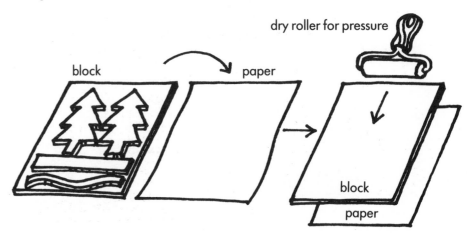

The raised card blocks can also be used for rubbings, either by gently rolling with a very lightly inked roller over the thin paper with the block underneath, or by the traditional method with a wax crayon (see figure 3).

Both techniques allow for overlaying colours. Take, for example, a Christmas bauble. Cut out a card in the shape of a bauble; look at the reflection lines and shapes, and cut similar shapes through the card; glue them in position; add some texture with embossed wallpapers and incise related line patterns using a pencil. Make multicoloured rubbings, trim and mount them on folded card.

Figure 3

lightly inked roller

paper

block

crayon rubbing

Finishing touches

These finishing touches should be an important part of the card-making process and not just last-minute jobs at the end of term. Children get great pleasure from doing as well as they can for a relatively short time.

Card messages

Happy Christmas

Age range
Five upwards.

Group size
Individuals.

What you need
Good quality white paper, pencils, coloured crayons, pens.

What to do
Give the children a piece of good white paper a little smaller than the card. It is much easier to produce satisfying work on this rather than the card itself.

Show them how to set out their writing and suggest leaving room for a border illustration, which could be as simple or as complicated as they like. Paper chains, crackers or a motif from their religious culture could be drawn carefully around the edges in pencil and carefully coloured with good pencil crayons or pastels. Even children who have only just learned how to write usually enjoy this activity.

The motif could reflect the design on the card and be repeated on the envelope, but most importantly it should be relevant to the child, either through personal experience or through work done in the classroom.

Making envelopes

Age range
Eight upwards.

Group size
Individuals.

What you need
An old envelope which has not been sealed, kitchen paper for practising, paper to make the envelope, glue.

What to do
Ask the pupils to take the envelope apart carefully to find out how it was made, then try to make one from the kitchen paper. Remember it will need to be a little bigger than the card, and don't forget to make allowances for sticking the flaps down.

Younger children can just fold up a rectangle of paper, which could be decorated round the edge for a special card.

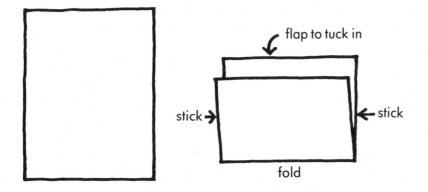

Christmas post-box

Age range
Five upwards.

Group size
Small groups.

What you need
Red card or shiny PVC material, glue or staples.

What to do
Ask a small group of children to make a post-box for the rest of the class to post their Christmas cards.

Make the card or PVC into a cylinder and staple or glue it together, discussing how the cylinder is made from the rectangle. Cut a circle of the same material, slightly bigger than the cylinder end. Cut across the radius and make it into a cone to fit the top of the cylinder, again talking about how the cone was made. Stick this on top of the cylinder, make a slit in the cylinder to push envelopes through, then stick a card on the front to give the collection times.

The post

Age range
Five upwards.

Group size
Whole class.

What you need
No special requirements.

What to do
Begin a classroom discussion by asking the children what happens to a letter or card after they have put it in the post-box. Discuss addresses and post-codes. They could make up post-codes for different parts of the school: for example, one part of the school could be N, a classroom in that area could be NL, and a particular part of the classroom could be given a number. Preceded by letters representing the school, a code might look like this: MGS NL2. All the areas in the school could have a post-code for the Christmas round.

This might develop an interest in having a post office in a corner of the classroom. This should include a 'parcel department' (a balance, and some lighter and heavier parcels), envelopes, cards, a stamp and ink pad and a sorting box. You may be able to persuade a local postman to come and talk about his work, or take the children to visit a sorting office (not too near Christmas!) Postman Pat stories also go down well with younger children.

Stamps

Age range
Five upwards.

Group size
Whole class.

What you need
Photocopy page 106.

What to do
Ask the class various questions like these: What are stamps for? Does anyone have a collection to show the others? What is the value of different stamps?

They could make up 18 pence worth of stamps in different ways, and design their own stamp for a festival (it need not be Christmas – Hong Kong have issued Chinese New Year stamps symbolising the year with its particular animal).

Give each child a copy of page 106 and ask them to work a design using felt-tipped pens or coloured crayons.

Encourage them to collect stamps from different parts of the world and display them with a map of the world, using string to match the stamp to its country of origin.

Try to make a collection of different Christmas stamps. The first stamp specifically issued for Christmas is said to have come from Canada in 1898, but they did not really become widespread until after World War II.

Parcel wrapping

The other major Christmas item dealt with by the Post Office is, of course, parcels, which usually contain presents to family and friends. Collect any relevant leaflets on parcel wrapping and addressing, as well as last dates for posting to different parts of the world.

Wrapping 'difficult' shapes

Age range
Five upwards.
(The object of the activity is to promote language and an awareness of shape, rather than train perfect parcel wrappers.)

Group size
Any size.

What you need
Three-dimensional shapes (eg cylinders, cubes, cuboids, spheres, spheroids, etc), wrapping paper, sticky tape, scissors.

What to do
Ask the children to select a shape to wrap. Why did they choose that particular one? What makes it more difficult to wrap some shapes than others? Is the paper big enough – or too big? What are the problems then? How can they be solved? Is there a particular way of dealing with the ends of the paper?

Choosing paper

Age range
Five upwards with help.

Group size
Any size.

What you need
Bulldog clips, different kinds of paper: eg strong brown paper, thin brown paper, kitchen paper, thin Christmas wrapping paper, tissue-paper, etc (the strips should all be the same length and the same widths as the clips), string, pebbles, a balance and a margarine pot (all the same size) for each strip of paper.

What to do
Show the children the equipment and ask them if they can devise a fair test to see which paper is strongest. Here is one way they can do it, but they may have other ideas which should be followed up.

Take one of the strips of paper and fold it in half. Clip the ends together with a bulldog clip.

Make two holes in the margarine pot just below the rim and thread string through one of the holes, tying a knot at the end. Thread the other end through the loop of paper and then through the second hole in the pot and tie another knot to hold it securely.

Suspend the clip on a hook, and put pebbles into the pot until the paper tears. (You could use weights with older children.) Label the pot and keep the pebbles in it until you have tried all the papers. Use the balance to determine which paper could hold the heaviest pot of pebbles. Repeat this test using damp paper to determine wet strength.

Christmas greenery

The holly and the ivy
When they are both full grown
Of all the trees that are in the wood,
The holly bears the crown.

Cecil J Sharp

IVY

HOLLY

Most of our Christmas customs can be traced back to long before the birth of Christ. When people began to celebrate Christmas, these ideas were taken on or sometimes adapted to symbolise Christian beliefs.

Evergreens have always played an important part in winter festivals. Homes were decorated with them because people believed that spirits must live in the leaves which were bright and green, when everything else appeared dead. Plants like holly, mistletoe and ivy were especially important because they have berries as well.

The word 'holly' probably comes from 'holy'; the prickly leaves remind Christians that Christ wore a crown of thorns on Good Friday and the red berries are seen as drops of His blood. (Romans used sprigs of holly as lucky tokens.)

Americans introduced the custom of putting wreaths of holly on their doors and windows. These are rather difficult for children to make, but a paper one is just as decorative.

Holly

Holly is now a symbol of Christmas, and with its shiny green leaves and lovely bright red berries it is a very attractive winter-time plant. It is often used to make decorations for the home during the festive period.

Holly wreaths

Age range
Five upwards.

Group size
Individuals.

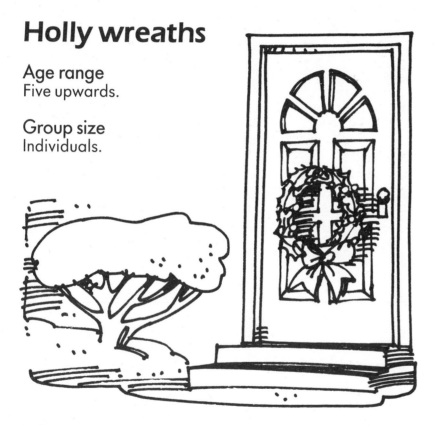

What you need
Thin card, scissors, glue, ruler, variety of papers (metallic, sticky, etc, in different greens), red metallic and sticky paper, a strip of red crêpe paper about 4 cm wide cut across the crêpe.

What to do
Ask the children to draw round something with a 30 cm diameter. From its centre draw a second circle, about 15 cm in diameter (see figure 1). Cut out both circles. (Younger children may need to have this done for them.)

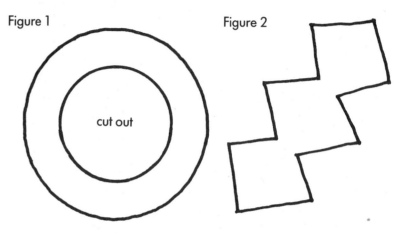

Figure 1

cut out

Figure 2

Cut out zigzags from green paper (in a variety of shades) to resemble holly leaves (see figure 2). Older children could study the holly leaf and copy it more accurately. Cut out red circles for the berries.

Figure 3

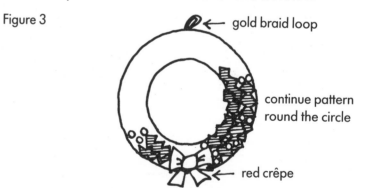

gold braid loop

continue pattern round the circle

red crêpe

Arrange the leaves and berries on the circle of card, overlapping the edges (see figure 3).

Holly leaves

Age range
Five upwards with some help.

Group size
Individuals, or small groups for younger children.

What you need
Rectangle of black sugar-paper about 20cm × 25cm, green tissue-paper, paste, scissors, chalk.

What to do
Give each child a rectangle of black sugar-paper and tell them to fold it in half lengthways. Start at the bottom left-hand corner and draw a zigzag with the chalk. Start again about 3 cm to the right and draw a second line, following the first (see figure 1). Younger children will need a careful demonstration.

Figure 1

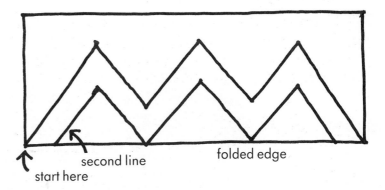

Now cut along the first and second lines, being very careful not to cut *along* the folded edge at either end. Open out the paper and paste along the edges before placing the tissue over it. When dry, any unwanted tissue can be trimmed away.

Older children may want to cut a curved line rather than a straight diagonal.

You could make red berries in a similar way and display both on windows (see figure 2).

Figure 2

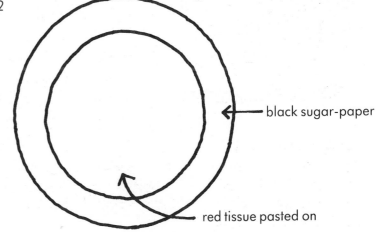

Clay leaves

Age range
Seven upwards.

Group size
Small groups.

What you need
Clay, rolling-pins, batons, clay tools.

What to do
First, ask the class to make some preliminary drawings of holly leaves. They should be large enough to show clearly the joints of the leaf curling upwards and the curved shapes between the points. Then roll out a rectangle of clay between the batons, about 25cm × 20cm. Lightly mark out the holly leaf and then carefully cut away from the outer edge, curving some of the points up and inwards. Mark the veins of the leaf.

When the leaves have been fired, they can be glazed with copper carbonate added to a transparent glaze.

Winter fairy frieze

Age range
Everyone could contribute to this.

Group size
Whole class.

What you need
Old gardening nets, greenery such as holly, ivy, etc, drawing materials, 'angel hair'.

What to do
String up old gardening nets and weave in real holly and ivy. Everyone can help to draw 'life-sized' fairies in light colours – pastels are good for this but any kind of crayon would do. Cut them out and display them among the greenery, then drape the frieze with 'angel hair' to give a more mysterious air. Use it as a basis for imaginative writing, which can be displayed with the drawings.

Edging

Age range
Seven upwards.

Group size
Any size.

What you need
Paper, chalk,
dark green paint,
PVA glue.

What to do
Draw outlines of holly leaves, about 20 to 25cm long.
Paint them and, when they are dry, cut them out. Cover
the leaves with the PVA glue to give a deep shine when
dry. These leaves are useful as an edging for a display or
to arrange in other ways: eg wreaths, holly bushes, etc,
for entrance halls and classrooms.

Mistletoe

Mistletoe was an ancient symbol, sacred to pre-Christian
Britain. It was supposed to be a 'truce' plant: where it
hung, enemies were ordered to stop fighting.

Back in the sixteenth century, Druids (Celtic magicians
and soothsayers) thought mistletoe was sacred and used
it in various customs.

Because the Druids used mistletoe, the Christian church
banned it, although it became quite popular to have
mistletoe in the home for decorative purposes.

Now, mistletoe is gathered at Christmas and people
arrange branches and sprigs of it in their homes. The
tradition of kissing under the mistletoe is supposed to be
lucky!

Observing and drawing mistletoe

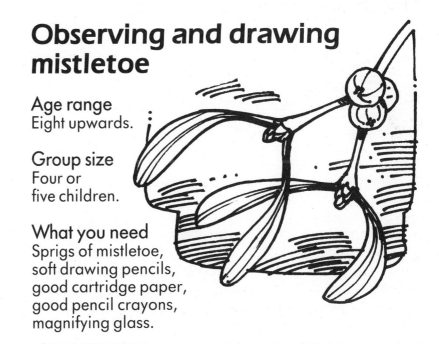

Age range
Eight upwards.

Group size
Four or
five children.

What you need
Sprigs of mistletoe,
soft drawing pencils,
good cartridge paper,
good pencil crayons,
magnifying glass.

What to do

Look for some mistletoe in the neighbourhood, but if there is none about, use reference books to find out how it grows. Bring some into the classroom – but remember that the berries are poisonous, so keep it out of reach unless an adult is supervising work.

Look carefully at the mistletoe – notice the distinctive shape of the leaves and how they are positioned on the stalk. Compare this with holly leaves: what difference is there between the colours of the leaves, as well as the obvious differences between the berries? What do the berries look like? Are they pure white or are there any other colours to be seen? Look at the leaves and berries under the magnifying glass. Draw the mistletoe – perhaps just one part of it – including as many of the observations as possible.

Mistletoe transfers

Age range
Seven or eight upwards.

Group size
Small groups.

What you need
White and green wax crayons, white paper (something a little stronger than kitchen paper), coloured sugar-paper or pastel paper, pencil, printing ink, small roller.

What to do
The children can cut the white paper to the size they want their design to be. Cover it fairly heavily with stripes of the white and green crayon. Turn the waxed side on to a piece of paper and, pressing heavily, draw the mistletoe design on the back. It will come through on to the coloured paper in green and white. You could finish this by thinly coating a small roller with printing ink in a complementary colour and lightly running it over the wax design on the coloured paper. This is a useful technique for Christmas cards and calendars.

Printing

Age range
Seven or eight upwards.

Group size
Small groups – quite a lot of room is necessary for printing to avoid mess and frustration.

What you need
Printing ink, newspaper, small roller, practice paper, tissue-paper.

What to do
Tell the children to practise on scrap paper before trying this on tissue-paper. Place a wad of newspaper under the paper they are going to print on. Carefully ink the mistletoe leaf, stalk, etc, and when they are in position on the paper, cover them with a folded sheet of newspaper and apply even pressure with a small roller. This could be used to make a repeat pattern on tissue-paper as a special piece of gift wrapping paper.

Experiment with other evergreens – scraps of fir tree would produce convincing Christmas trees, for example.

Christmas trees

Like holly, ivy and mistletoe, the Christmas tree has been about in different forms long before it became associated with Christmas. Romans used to decorate their temples with evergreen branches during winter festivals and, at the Festival of the Kalends, they exchanged fronds of evergreen as we exchange presents.

From the early Middle Ages the yule log was brought into English houses to burn throughout the yule festival. In Devon, instead of a yule log they used a bundle of faggots tied with nine bands of green ash. Each unmarried girl chose a band; the one who chose the band which burned first would be the first to marry the following year.

Before the nineteenth century, people often hung branches of yew and holly from their ceilings, sometimes decorated with ribbons, fruit and sweets. Wealthy families in Britain, including the Victorian royal family, introduced the German custom of decorating the tree, and soon it became common practice to put candles, ribbons, sweets, etc, on the branches. Nowadays, of course, dangerous candles have been replaced by electric lights, and coloured baubles and tinsel are used.

Most Christmas trees brought inside are spruce, lodgepole pine, noble fir and Scots pine. The tree which stands in Trafalgar Square each Christmas is a Norwegian spruce, sent from Norway by way of thanks for Britain's struggle in the World War II.

Observing Christmas trees

Age range
Five upwards.

Group size
Whole class.

What you need
Paints, magnifying glasses, tissue-paper, samples of pine cones, pine needles, holly leaves.

What to do
Take your class to a park, if possible, to study the different kinds of conifer. Get them to collect some of the needles and identify them by using reference books. They will notice that Christmas trees are symmetrical, and the true Christmas tree, the Norwegian spruce, has a very distinctive colour. Ask the children to try to mix the colour themselves, and compare it with the colours of other evergreens.

Leaves
Christmas trees are 'needle-leaved'. Discuss the differences between the Christmas tree's needles and other common leaves. Start by rolling a needle between finger and thumb, then lead up to cutting a needle across, to see the shape of its cross-section. This is better seen with a good magnifying glass.

Then look at a holly leaf carefully, and compare it with the needle; they both have hard edges and sharp tips. Ask if the children can suggest reasons for leaves which last through the winter surviving better if they have hard edges and sharp points. The way spruce needles are arranged on the twig is not a common pattern. Looked at from underneath, the twig looks as if it has a centre-parting, while the needles on top of the twig point outwards and forwards.

The needles have a special smell, too. Try folding a few in a tissue, hammering them (not too hard), then smelling them. The oil in the needles makes them burn more easily than juicy leaves, so it is important to keep light bulbs, and especially candle flames, well away from them. It is far better *not* to have candles on the tree!

Seeds
What is special about the seeds of the Norwegian spruce? You can't find this out from an ordinary Christmas tree, because it will probably have been uprooted before it is old enough to have any seeds. However, the children may know that needle-leaved trees have cones instead of fruits. The scales on the outside of a cone are smooth, and overlap in a beautiful spiral (helix) pattern. If you are lucky or clever enough to get some of the seeds from between the scales of a ripe cone, they can be grown in the spring. Instead of producing two first leaves, as beans do, they start with a bunch of seven thin green needles. If you buy a tree with roots, replant it.

Tissue-paper Christmas trees

Age range
Six or seven upwards.

Group size
Small groups
for younger children.

What you need
Rectangle of black paper about 30cm × 20cm, green tissue-paper, scissors, paste, chalk.

What to do
Use the same technique as for the 'Holly leaves' (see page 39). Fold the rectangle in half lengthways with the fold on the left-hand side. Start at the top left-hand corner and draw an outline of a Christmas tree. Then about 3cm below the starting point of the first line, draw a second

Figure 1

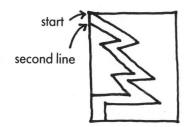

line, but do not follow the first line down the tree trunk (see figure 1).

Carefully cut along both lines, making sure you *don't cut along the fold*. Open out the tree, paste along the inner edges, and back it with green tissue. The inner tree shape which will come from the middle could be decorated with shiny scraps of paper and sequins.

Christmas prints

Age range
Five upwards.

Group size
Individuals.

What you need
Spruce-coloured paint mixed fairly thickly, brushes, paper (perhaps a slightly different green)

What to do
Fold the paper in half with the fold down the left-hand side (see figure 1).

Figure 1

Open the paper out and paint thick downward strokes in the outline of a tree on one side only (see figure 2).

Figure 2

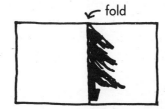

Fold the paper over again and press down hard. Open it up and the tree will have printed itself on the second side of the paper. You can cut it out when dry and mount it on a suitable background.

45

Tree decorations

During the 130 years or so that we have been using Christmas tree decorations in this country, they have changed from ribbons, candles and sweets to tinsel, baubles and electric lights. But, however sophisticated commercial decorations have become, children still enjoy making their own, and it is often these that reappear year after year as part of the family traditions. There are endless ways of making these decorations, so here are just two which can be made simply and inexpensively.

Dough decorations

Age range
Six upwards.

Group size
Small groups.

What you need
A cup of salt,
a cup of flour,
water, cooking oil,
paints, varnish,
PVA glue,
thread or ribbon,
felt scraps.

What to do

Give each group a set of ingredients and ask them to mix together the salt and flour, then add enough water to make a stiff paste. Some cooking oil can be added to make the dough more manageable.

Use the dough to make tree decorations, but do not make them very large or they will be too heavy to hang up. Stick two balls of dough together with a little water to make snowmen, or make a Christmas pudding from a single ball.

Bake the decorations in a cool oven until the dough has set, then paint and varnish them. Stick on felt scarves, hats, leaves, etc, and finish off with a loop of thread for hanging the decoration on the tree.

Flattened circles can be used to make Christmas tree-shaped and star-shaped brooches, baking and painting them in the same way as the snowmen and puddings. Thread a safety pin through a circle of felt before sticking it to the back of the dough shape.

Gingerbread shapes

Age range
Six upwards with help.

Group size
Small groups.

What you need
A fairly thin slab of cooked gingerbread, card, a knife or biscuit cutters, a knitting needle, icing sugar.

What to do
Using biscuit cutters or a knife, cut out shapes such as hearts, stars or trees from the gingerbread. Younger children may need help. Make an icing sugar and water mix to decorate the shapes. Push a knitting needle through the top of each one, and thread narrow ribbon through to make a hanging loop.

Festive candles

Little Nancy Etticoat,
In a white petticoat
And a red nose;
The longer she stands
The shorter she grows.

Anon

Because people used to believe that the sun was a god which left them in winter time, they built fires to give the god strength to return with the heat and light of summer. So long before Christmas celebrations were initiated, fire played an important part in annual rituals. Christians later took the flame as a symbol of truth — hence the significance of candles in churches.

The candle eventually became part of the Christmas ritual and was usually lit on Christmas Eve. It was supposed to burn all through the night. The remains of the candle were kept throughout the year to protect against bad luck. One legend tells us that Martin Luther first put candles on a Christmas tree as a reminder of the stars that shone above Bethlehem when Jesus was born.

A project on candles could start with a collection of different kinds of candle (eg birthday candles, household candles, church candles, coloured dinner candles, tapers, night lights, etc), and a discussion about their particular uses. (It is important to stress the dangers of lighted candles and matches.)

Examining candles

Children will find a project on candles fascinating. It lends itself to simple scientific experiments as well as enjoyable craft work. Remember to supervise the children when matches and candles are used.

Observing candles

Age range
Five upwards with careful supervision.

Group size
Small groups.

What you need
Candle, matches, paints, palettes, brushes, paper.

What to do
This activity must be very closely supervised by an adult. Light the candle and ask the children to look at the shape of the flame. Does it change shape as you watch? If so, what caused that to happen? Is the flame just one colour? Note the change of colour from the wick to the edge of the flame. What makes them different?

Ask the children to paint the flame *only*, making it touch the top and bottom of the paper. They should try to mix the colours that can be seen in the flame. This can be developed by older children into a design for print work with a stencil or 'glue block' (see pages 50 and 51).

Stencil candle flame

Age range
Ten to twelve.

Group size
Individuals.

What you need
Craft knife, thin card, ready-mixed Tempera paint, stencilling brush.

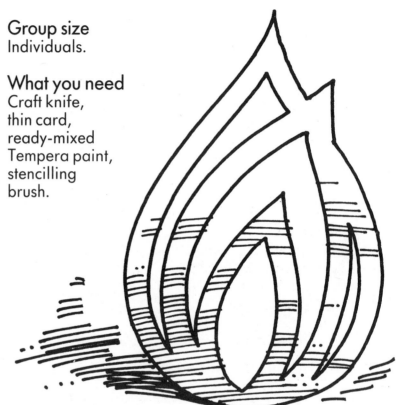

What to do
Get the class to draw a candle flame design on thin card, based on earlier observation.

Carefully cut away the white parts with a craft knife. Place the stencil on paper and block in the colour with the stencil brush. The children could use these as a repeat pattern for wrapping paper or for a card design.

Glue prints

Age range
Eight upwards.

Group size
Small groups.

What you need
Wood glue in a plastic container with a nozzle,
a block of wood or hardboard about 10cm square,
a piece of chalk,
printing ink and rollers or wax crayons.

What to do
The children should draw a candle design on to wood using a piece of chalk, then follow the lines with glue. Do not spread the glue – just allow it to settle. When it has hardened completely, the block can be used for rubbings with wax crayon, or inked up with printing ink to make prints.

Tissue flames

Age range
Seven to nine.

Group size
Individuals or
two to four children
working together.

What you need
Yellow and
red tissue-paper,
scissors,
paste.

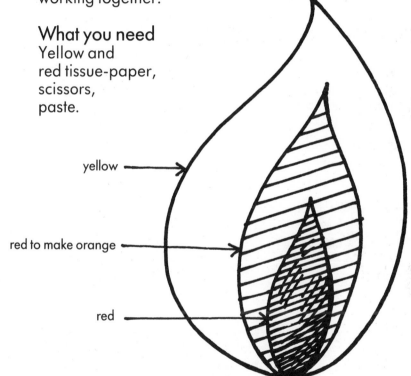

yellow

red to make orange

red

What to do
Cut 'flames' in different sizes from the yellow and red tissue-paper. Starting with the biggest yellow one, arrange them on top of each other to produce the effect of colour change.

51

Candle burning

Age range
Eight to ten.

Group size
Small groups.

What you need
Household candle, ruler, clock stamp, photocopy page 107.

What to do
Get each group to measure the candle and make a careful note of its length. Light it, out of a draught, first thing in the morning. Measure it every half hour and keep a note of the results. How long does it take to burn away? Does it burn the same amount each hour? Would a 'candle clock' be reliable?

The findings could be recorded on the photocopied sheet.

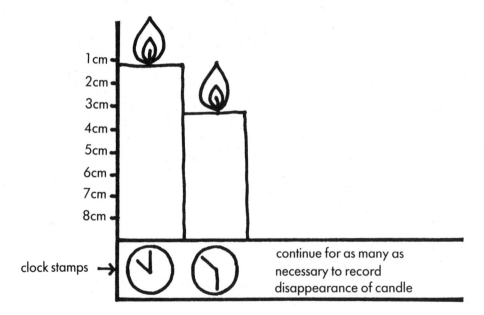

clock stamps →

continue for as many as necessary to record disappearance of candle

Candle alarm clock

Age range
Nine upwards.

Group size
Small groups of two to four children.

What you need
Candle, cotton, pins, elastic bands, Plasticine, tin lids, string, plastic pot lids, etc.

What to do
When the children have found out how long it takes to burn a candle (see page 52), provide them with the materials listed above and ask them to make an alarm clock. Obviously not all the materials will be suitable, but the children should make their own selection. This selection process is an important part of the work.

What is a candle?

Age range
Seven upwards.

Group size
Any size, but the activity involves a lighted candle.

What you need
A small candle (eg a birthday cake candle) for each group, matches, pencils, paper photocopy pages 108 and 109.

What to do
Tell each group that they are aliens from outer space visiting Earth. They find an object, the candle, and are trying to report back to their planet since their people might find it useful. They have to write down ten observations.

Now light it and write down ten observations while it is burning. When it has burned out, they can write down anything else observed, then look at the lists and talk about the senses used in the observation. Allocate points for each observation involving sight, touch, hearing, and smell. (Note: Do not encourage the children to *taste* unknown things.)

Deduct a point for everything not strictly observed: for example, that it is made of wax. Add a point for every quantification: for example, that it is as long as my little finger.

Add up the score at the end and discuss with the children how their observations involved more than just sight. Talk about the 'describing' words they found for texture, smell and hearing.

Put the candle out

Age range
Ten to twelve.

Group size
Small groups.

What you need
For each group: three candle stumps, three saucers, three different-sized jars, stop clock.

What to do
Light the three candles. Ask each group to devise a way of extinguishing the candles simultaneously by putting the jars over them in sequence.

Making candles

Working with hot wax can be dangerous, so when making candles an adult should always be present. Wax must be heated in a double boiler – never over an open flame – and an asbestos mat can be placed over the gas flame as an added precaution. The wax should be heated slowly and never left unattended, and a thermometer should be used to control the temperature. Keep water away from molten wax as it can cause spitting and may fracture the candle if it gets into the mould. If the wax does ignite, smother the flames with a cloth or pan lid, and not water.

Christmas candle

Age range
Ten to twelve.

Group size
Two or three children.

What you need
A double boiler and a separate container, 20 tablespoons granulated paraffin wax, a thermometer, about 20cm of wicking, a commercially made cylindrical mould 10cm high by 6cm in diameter, Plasticine, pencil, ⅛ red dye disc, 2 tablespoons stearin, cooling bath, skewer, craft knife.

What to do
In groups, melt the wax in the double boiler. Knot one end of the wick, then dip the whole wick in the hot wax and pull it straight while it is still pliable. Thread it through the base of the mould and seal over the knot on the outside with Plasticine. Pull the wick taut and tie the free end tightly to a pencil placed centrally across the top of the mould, to prevent the wick from wilting when the hot wax is poured (see figure 1).

Figure 1

wick

pencil

Using a separate container in the double boiler, dissolve the dye in stearin, then add it to the melted wax and reheat. Pour the wax into the centre of the mould to within 1cm of the top, reserving a little for topping up (see figure 2).

Figure 2

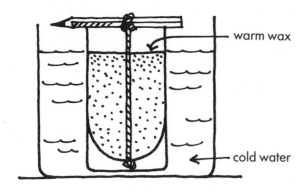

warm wax

cold water

Let the wax stand for a few minutes, then tap the sides of the mould gently to release any air bubbles. Stand the mould in a bath of cold water with the water level the same as that of the wax. Weight the mould to hold it down.

After 15 minutes, check to see if a well has appeared around the wick. If so, break the surface skin of the wax with a skewer and top up round the wick with melted wax

Figure 3

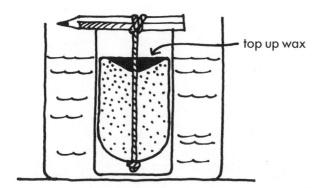

top up wax

(see figure 3). Do not overfill when topping up or the wax will run to the sides and form a wedge between the mould and the candle, making it difficult to remove (see figure 4). This process may have to be repeated.

Return the mould to the cold water bath to harden. When the candle has cooled over a period of several hours, remove the seal from the base of the mould, turn it upside down and tap it gently so that the candle slides out. If it is difficult to remove, stand the mould in a refrigerator for half an hour, then try again. Trim the wick and level the base of the candle with a craft knife.

Figure 4

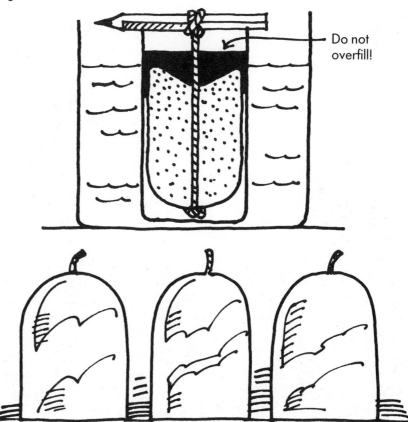

Do not overfill!

Floating boats

Age range
Six upwards with help.

Group size
Small groups.

What you need
A sharp knife,
walnuts, wax,
stearin and dye mix
as for moulded candle,
wicking,
non-flammable adhesive,
a matchstick,
an egg-box,
a dish of water.

What to do
Using a sharp knife, halve the walnuts and remove the contents of each shell. (The teacher should do this before commencing the project.) Heat the wax and cut the wick into 4cm lengths.

Knot one end of each piece of wick, dip it in wax and pull it straight. Place a blob of adhesive centrally in the base of each nutshell and push the knotted end of the wick on to the adhesive with the help of a matchstick, so that the wicks stand up vertically. Stand the shells in an egg-box and leave the adhesive to dry.

Fill the shells with wax and allow it to set before topping up round the wicks. When completed, the walnut boats can be floated in a shallow dish filled with water.

Note: It is important to use non-flammable adhesive that will not exude toxic fumes when heated.

Orange peel lanterns

Figure 1

Age range
Five upwards
with a little help.

Group size
Small groups.

What you need
Thick-skinned oranges,
a sharp pointed knife,
a spoon,
narrow wicking,
small metal washers,
vegetable cooking oil.

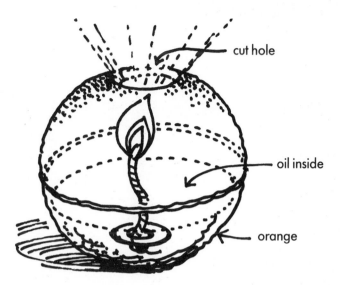

What to do
Cut each orange horizontally into two halves, and scoop
out the flesh using a spoon, without damaging the peel.
Cut a circle, 2.5cm in diameter, from the centre of one
half. (An adult should prepare the oranges for younger
children.) Cut a 5cm length of wicking, knot one end and
pull it through the washer. Position the wick centrally on
the bottom half of the orange and half fill the skin with
vegetable oil. Light the wick and place the top cover in
position (see figure 1).

cut hole

oil inside

orange

These are simple for younger children to make and
they look most effective grouped round the tree or on the
Christmas table.

Shining stars

Twinkle, twinkle little star
How I wonder what you are
Up above the world so high
Like a diamond in the sky.

The star is an important symbol at Christmas-time; we are told that a star indicated Jesus' birth, and it has since become a focus of many favourite songs and carols, as well as being featured strongly in Christmas decorations.
It would be easy for children to imagine that stars are simply the perfect geometric shape they encounter at Christmas-time. So a good starting point for a project on stars would be to ask children what they think stars are, and how they got up in the sky. The explanation that a star is a mass of burning gases might well emerge with the help of books and teacher guidance.

Sky at night

A good basis for a project on stars is the sky at night. Encourage discussion and work on the constellations – most children will find this fascinating.

Burning gases

Age range
Five to twelve.

Group size
Individuals.

What you need
Powdered inks in a variety of colours, glitter, scraps of shiny paper, silver and/or gold spray paint, Marvin medium, white paper 50cm × 30cm.

What to do
Discuss with the whole class what colours might be seen in burning gases. Talk about hot colours, white heat, etc. Look at pictures of the Milky Way and Van Gogh's *Starry Night*, and encourage discussion about pattern.

Get them to cover the paper with different colours using the diluted ink and spray paint. When it is dry, add pattern detail in glitter and small scraps of paper. Let the glue harden and then cover the pattern with Marvin medium. (This will intensify the colour and provide a deep shine.) Display the work double-mounted on gold or silver and black paper.

Milky Way galaxy

Age range
Six to nine.

Group size
Individuals.

What you need
25cm square of white paper, powdered inks, glitter, scissors, glue.

What to do
Cover the paper and add detail as for 'Burning gases' (page 60), but don't coat the pattern with Marvin medium. When the ink and glue are dry, cut the paper into a spiral. Reconstruct the spiral on dark background paper leaving spaces between the curves (see figure 1).

A larger galaxy could be made as a group project and used as a background for displaying writing about stars, or star Haiku (see page 67).

Figure 1

Follow-up
Look for spirals in other natural forms and make a book containing pictures or drawings of them. Investigate how the spiral is useful in everyday life.

Free painting

Age range
Five upwards.

Group size
Any size.

What you need
Music, paints, paper.

What to do
Play music such as Holst's *Planet Suite* as a stimulus for free painting work. Provide a choice of paper, colour and size, as well as a variety of paints, palettes, sponge and brushes. It is interesting to see what paintings the music inspires.

Making stars

Extend the project work on the sky at night to include making different types of stars. The ones we have given range from the simple to the more complicated for older, more able pupils.

Individual stars

Age range
Six to nine.

Group size
Individuals.

What you need
White paper (preferably with a 'finish'), silver, blue and purple wax crayons and a blue 'wash' (powdered ink diluted works well or a very thin powder paint mix), or gold, red, orange and yellow wax crayons with a red or yellow wash, pencils, scissors.

What to do
Get the children to draw a star to touch the top, bottom and sides of a piece of paper. (Don't worry about the number of points or perfect formation.)

Cut out the star (see figure 1), then starting in the middle, begin to make a circular pattern with a wax crayon. Surround it with another pattern in a different colour. Continue until the star is covered (see figure 2). Encourage the children to press hard.

Figure 1   Figure 2

When the pattern is complete, cover it in wash. These can be displayed on threads as a mobile (in which case, decorate both sides) or stuck/stapled on to a dark background.

A perfect eight-pointed star

Age range
Six upwards.

Group size
Individuals.

What you need
A square of any kind
of paper or material,
scissors, crayons, glitter, glue.

What to do
Fold the square into quarters (see figure 1),

Figure 1

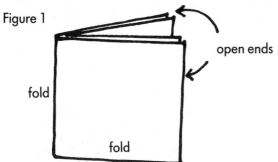

and then into eighths (see figure 2),

Figure 2

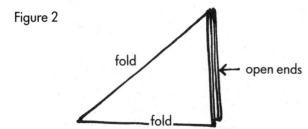

and then sixteenths. Make a diagonal cut from right to left as shown (see figure 3).

Figure 3

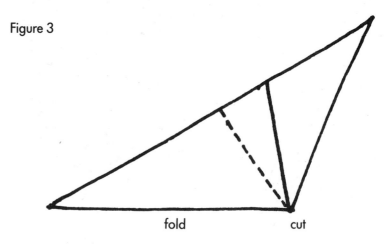

Open this out into a star. You can vary the length of the points by the angle of the cut. Decorate the star with crayons and glitter.

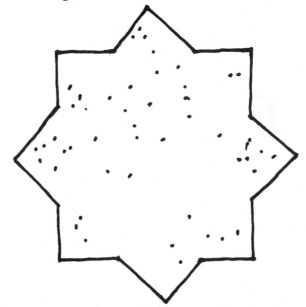

A three-dimensional star

Age range
Ten to twelve.

Group size
Individuals, or
six children can
produce one between them.

What you need
Good quality
cartridge paper
or thin white card,
a ruler,
pencils,
a craft knife or
scissors,
glue.

What to do
Start with a 5cm cube. Make five pyramids, each with a 5cm base and 10cm edges (see figure 1).

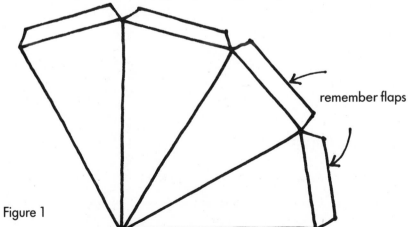

remember flaps

Figure 1

Attach pyramids to five sides of the cube. Make a sixth pyramid with a 5cm base but 20cm edges to fix to the sixth side (see figure 2).

Figure 2

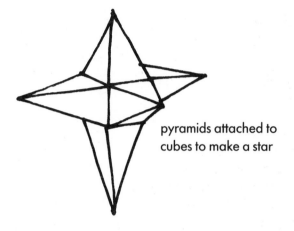

pyramids attached to
cubes to make a star

Much larger stars can be made, but keep the proportions 5:10:20. This produces a good shape which is reasonably rigid. Large stars make very good hall decorations.

63

Folded star

Age range
Seven upwards.

Group size
Individuals or pairs.

What you need
Two squares of stiff paper (foil wrapping paper is good), glue, scissors.

What to do
Pleat both squares like a fan. When they are folded into strips, cut points at the edges. Fold each one in half and glue the edges together (see figure 1).

Figure 1

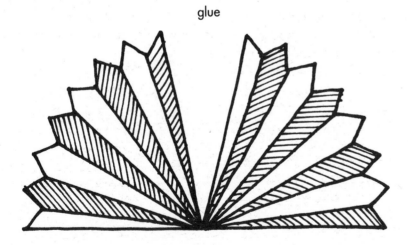

glue

Then glue both fans together (see figure 2).

Figure 2

glue →   ← glue

Clay stars

Age range
Six to nine.

Group size
Small groups.

What you need
Clay,
batons,
rolling-pins,
clay tools.

What to do

Ask the groups to make some preliminary drawings of stars. It doesn't matter about perfect formation or the precise number of points. The points should not be too thin or the clay will crack.

Roll the clay (about 1cm thick) between two batons of equal depth (see figure 1). Mark out the star using the

Figure 1

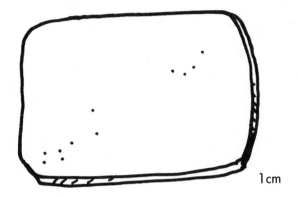

1cm

drawings as a guide. Then carefully cut away the clay from the outside edge (see figure 2). (Younger children might need a little help here.) Use the clay tools to make a design on the star, then bake and glaze it with an

Figure 2

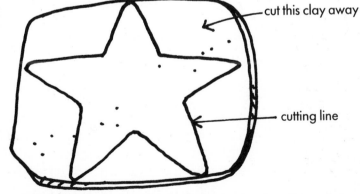

cut this clay away

cutting line

opaque white glaze and cobalt carbonate detail to give a milky blue/white effect.

Star biscuits

Age range
Five upwards with help.

Group size
Four children.

What you need
180g flour,
60g sugar,
120g margarine,
rolling-pin,
mixing bowl,
scales,
pastry board,
cutters or
cardboard shapes,
baking tray,
icing sugar,
'hundreds and thousands',
gold and silver balls.

What to do
Mix the flour with the sugar. Rub in the margarine until the crumbs are evenly sized and can be pressed together to make a soft dough. Roll it out thinly (about 1cm or less) and cut it into star shapes. Put the biscuits on a lightly greased tray and bake them for about ten minutes at 350°F/180°C/gas mark 4, until they are lightly browned. Mix a little icing sugar with some water and decorate the biscuits. Add 'hundreds and thousands' and some gold and silver balls.

Star writing patterns

Age range
Five to nine.

Group size
Any size.

What you need
Squared paper (larger squares are more suitable for younger children), gold and silver pencils or crayons.

What to do
Demonstrate how to make a star in one square. Make sure the children understand where the corners are, what 'top' means, and so on.

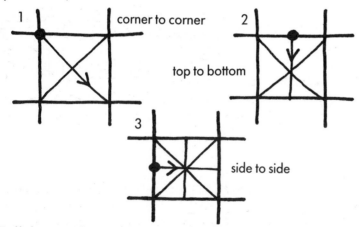

Tell them to begin at the top left-hand corner (make a dot for younger children) and draw a line to the opposite corner. (You will need to do this as you're explaining it.) Then repeat from the top right-hand corner. Continue, from top to bottom and side to side, making sure each line touches its starting and finishing point. Draw one star in gold, the next in silver, and so on to the end of the line.

Get the groups to make up some more Christmas patterns in the squares: for example, green zigzags and red circles. They must make sure that all their patterns touch the edges of the squares.

Star poems

Age range
Eight to twelve.

Group size
Individuals.

What you need
No special requirements.

What to do
Discuss and read a selection of star poems. Suggest to the children that they might enjoy writing some star poems of their own.

Forcing a rhyme on a poem is difficult to do and often results in a strangely stilted style. Haiku is a Japanese form of poetry. Each consists of 17 syllables, generally arranged as a line of five, a line of seven and a line of five. They don't usually rhyme which makes them easier to write, and they also provide a manageable opportunity for children to work at a piece of writing without being overwhelmed by the task.

Here are some attempts at Haiku:

Millions of miles away
Stars blaze in the evening sky
Will they shoot tonight?

After quite a lot of work on the sun and trying several
Haiku, a seven-year-old wrote:

The sun set
Each night when there's no light
The sun goes down under the ground
But where does it go?
What does it do?
It probably just has a snooze zzzzzzzz
Matthew Lemmon

Suggest that the children design their own
backgrounds to illustrate the poems – the eight-pointed
star might be a starting point. Use the poems as an
opportunity for children to present their best work. The
poems can either be incorporated into the design or
written out separately and then stuck on.

Ideas for decorating stars

Here are a few different ideas for decorating the stars
that have been made. Remember to supervise the
children at all times when melting the candle wax for the
batik stars.

Batik

Age range
Eight to twelve
with close supervision.

Group size
Individuals.

What you need
Cut-out stars, candles and matches, spring clothes pegs,
tray of black or coloured ink (*not* paint), newspaper, iron,
felt-tipped pens.

What to do
Light the candle and very carefully drop melted wax over
the star. Run it under cold water until it is set and brittle.
Carefully crumple the waxed star, open it out and
immerse it in a tray of ink, holding the star with a clothes
peg. Leave it for ten minutes, then remove it and let it
drip dry.
Iron the star between sheets of newspaper until the wax
is removed. When it has all gone, the white areas can be
blocked in with felt-tipped pens – pinks, oranges and
reds work well.

Marbling

Age range
Five to twelve
younger children will
need supervision.

Group size
Two or three children.

What you need
Cut-out stars,
marbling inks
and droppers,
tray of water,
newspaper.

What to do
Each group should fill a tray with water and put one or
two drops of different-coloured marbling inks on the
surface. Carefully swirl them around, then place a star on
the surface and pull it out at the other end of the tray.
Gold and silver enamel modelling paints look good if
they are well diluted with white spirit.

Sewing stars

Age range
Six to twelve.

Group size
Individuals.

What you need
Felt stars,
a variety of threads,
sequins, needles, glue.

What to do
The stars can be decorated with any kind of free stitching
and sequins, then mounted on card or backed with a
contrasting colour in felt.

The sun

The sun is the nearest and most important star; it provides
us with all our light and governs our seasons. Long
before Christianity, people used to worship the sun.

The shortest day of the year was 25 December when
there was less sunlight than any other day and people
prayed to the sun to return for another summer. Now we
use a different calendar and the shortest day falls on 21
December.

A sun frieze

Age range
Six upwards.

Group size
Individuals or
twos and threes
for larger friezes.

What you need
Squares of black sugar-paper (50cm square is about right), red, orange and yellow paint, red, orange, yellow and gold oil pastels.

What to do
Remind the children that the sun is a mass of boiling gas. (Chapter 5 of *The Iron Man* by Ted Hughes gives an excellent description of this.) Ask them to begin roughly in the centre of the paper and make strokes towards the edges, first discussing the different strokes that could be made (long, short, thick, thin, zigzags, broken lines, stripes, and so on), and the use of colours together.

Allow the paint to dry and then add more (radial) pattern with the oil pastels; encourage the children to work as boldly as possible. They may have other ideas about additions to the pattern, which could become the basis for collage. Display the 'suns' side by side.

Sew a sun!

Age range
Six upwards.

Group size
Individuals.

What you need
A square of hessian (about 20cm) in red, yellow or orange, different kinds of thread and wool in the same colour range plus gold, sequins, sewing needles, glue, card, calendars.

What to do
Start roughly in the centre of the hessian and work radial patterns in any kind of stitching. Children will have their own ideas: zigzags, over-stitching – anything that catches their fancy. Encourage colour variety and provide sequins if the children would like them. Mount the hessian on to card, and add a gold loop and a calendar.

Fun and games

Ask no questions
Tell no lies
Ever seen mincemeat
in mince pies?

Michael Rosen

The school Christmas party is usually organised by staff and parents, but it can provide some very useful learning in the classroom. Even if you are holding a party for the whole school, individual classes or areas might like to organise their own by way of a thank-you to those who have helped over the year, for local old people, or for anyone else they may be involved with.

The children could plan and cook food, do the shopping, organise games, make hats, crackers and masks, and send invitations as part of their classwork. Even quite small children could carry out the majority of this work with support.

Papier mâché food

Age range
Six upwards
with some help.

Group size
About six children.

What you need
Paper plates,
newspaper,
kitchen paper,
paste,
paint,
PVA glue.

What to do
Discuss with the class what kind of food they would like
on their perfect party plate! What shapes would they be?
What colours?

Tell them to mix the paste to a fairly thick, but not solid
consistency and tear the newspaper into small strips,
about 10cm × 5cm. Screw or fold the newspaper to the
appropriate shape and cover it with a layer of paste.
Stick small pieces of newspaper over this, making sure it
is well pasted down. Make several layers like this,
finishing with a layer of white kitchen paper.

Leave the shapes to dry and then paint them in the
appropriate colours. The children could have great fun
painting exotic cakes. Coat all the items with PVA glue
and, when they are dry, glue them securely to the paper
plate. This could be displayed with some writing about
party food.

Sandwich graph

Age range
All ages.

Group size
Any size.

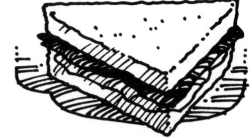

What you need
5cm square of plain white paper for each child, coloured
sugar-paper, photocopy page 110.

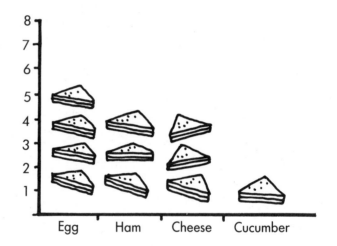

What to do
Ask everyone to draw a picture of their favourite
sandwich and write underneath what it is (non-writers
can have this done for them).

As a group activity ask each children to stick their
drawing on to the sugar-paper to form a graph, and find
out the most and least popular sandwiches. Use this as a
basis for some mathematical work: for example, are
there more cucumber than egg sandwiches, and if so,
how many more?

Party crackers

Age range
Five upwards with help.

Group size
Small groups.

What you need
A cardboard tube,
crêpe paper,
white paper,
felt-tipped pens,
scraps of metallic
paper,
sweets,
greaseproof
paper.

crêpe
paper

cardboard
tube

What to do
Wrap a sweet or little biscuit in a piece of greaseproof
paper, and put it into the cardboard tube with a joke or
riddle written by the children. Roll the crêpe paper
around the tube, twist both ends, and fringe or curl the
tips. Stick a little drawing on the top of the cracker and
decorate it with metallic paper shapes.

Party games

Age range
All ages.

Group size
Any size.

What you need
Photocopy page 111.

What to do
Ask the children what their favourite party games are.
There may be some that others don't know, especially if
you have children from different parts of the country or of
a different ethnic origin. Get them to ask their parents
and grandparents what games they used to play at
parties. Then suggest they choose a game, write down
instructions explaining how to play it and provide some
illustrations. Practise the games before the party so that
everyone understands what to do.
   You could make a frieze of party games, and perhaps
another of games children played at Christmas in
Victorian or some other time past.

Party food

Children will love to make their own food for the party. Remember to supervise them at all times, particularly when they are using the oven.

Biscuits from Finland

Age range
Five upwards with help.

Group size
Small groups.

What you need
150g plain flour,
75g brown sugar,
100g margarine,
½ teaspoon almond essence.

What to do
In Finland, tiny biscuits, cut in a variety of shapes – stars, hearts, circles, little people, crescents – are baked and bundled up, a few at a time, in bright paper tied with ribbon. These bundles are used as small gifts and could be given at the end of the party to take home.

Mix all the ingredients together by hand to make a rollable dough. Roll it out thinly and cut it into shapes using biscuit cutters or a knife. Bake the biscuits for 15 to 20 minutes at about 335°F/180C/gas mark 4. This makes about 25 small biscuits.

Biscuit decorations from Northern Europe

Age range
Five upwards with help.

Group size
Small groups.

What you need
200g plain or self-raising flour,
50g fat,
½ cup water.

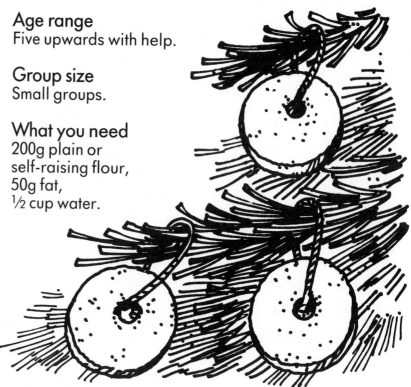

What to do
These small biscuits are baked with holes in them so you could hang them on the Christmas tree. If the biscuits are going to be eaten fairly soon, the recipe for 'Biscuits from Finland' (page 74) can be used. However, originally the biscuits were baked to hang on trees outside as a gift for the birds. If you want to do this, use this recipe.

Mix all the ingredients to a dough and roll it out fairly thinly. Cut it into rounds and make a small hole in the middle of each round. Bake the biscuits in a hot oven, 450°F/230°C/gas mark 8, for about ten minutes.

West Indian bakes

Age range
Five upwards with help.

Group size
Small groups.

What you need
200g plain flour,
50g fat,
1 teaspoon salt,
2 teaspoons baking powder,
1 teaspoon sugar,
4 to 6 tablespoons water
or coconut milk.

What to do
Dissolve the sugar in two tablespoons of water or coconut milk in a small bowl. Sift the flour, salt and baking powder into another bowl, then rub in the fat. Make a well in the mixture and add the sugar liquid. Add the remaining water or coconut milk slowly until a soft dough is formed. Knead the dough gently, and shape it into rounds when smooth. Prick all over and bake at 400°F/200°C/gas mark 6 until golden brown (about 30 minutes). Serve them hot or cold.

Burfi from India

Age range
Five upwards with help.

Group size
Small groups.

What you need
2 packets
dessicated coconut,
1 cup sugar,
3 cups water,
1 large tin
evaporated milk.

What to do
This sweetmeat is eaten at special events. It is usually made from full cream dried milk (*khoa*) but evaporated milk can be used as a substitute. Many variations can be made by using fruit, nuts, cardamom, etc.

Mix the coconut with the evaporated milk. Boil the water and sugar together until they thicken, then lower the heat and add the coconut mixture. Add the butter slowly, stirring all the time. Allow the mixture to thicken and add nuts, fruit or any other flavouring. Spread the mixture on to a greased shallow tin or plate. Wait a few minutes until it starts to set, then mark it into squares and leave it to cool.

Christmas tree biscuits

Age range
Five upwards with help.

Group size
Small groups.

What you need
For biscuits:
200g flour,
100g margarine,
100g soft brown sugar,
1 pinch ground ginger,
50g treacle,
50g golden syrup.
For icing:
100g icing sugar,
½ tablespoon orange or lemon juice.

What to do
Pre-heat the oven to 375°F/190°C/gas mark 5. Sift the flour into a large bowl. Add all the other ingredients and work the mixture with your hands until you have an evenly coloured dough. Flour a board and your rolling-pin, and roll out the dough to about 3mm thickness.

Cut out the biscuits, put them on a greased baking sheet and bake them on the middle shelf for 20 minutes until lightly browned. Allow them to cool on a wire rack.

Make some icing by sieving 100g of icing sugar into a bowl. Heat half a tablespoon of water and mix it with half a tablespoon of orange or lemon juice. Add a little at a time to the icing sugar, beating well until the icing coats the spoon and is shiny. Add colouring, if desired, and decorate the biscuits with currants, silver balls and pieces of chopped glacé cherries.

Peppermint creams

Age range
Five upwards with help.

Group size
Small groups.

What you need
200g icing sugar,
peppermint essence,
1 egg white,
cooking chocolate.

What to do
Separate one egg and put the white into a large bowl. Whip the egg white until it is light and frothy, and gradually beat in the sifted icing sugar.

Sugar a board or table-top and put the mixture on it. Pour on half a teaspoon of peppermint essence and knead the mixture. When it seems firm and dry roll it out with a rolling-pin and cut it into small rounds with the smallest biscuit cutter or an upturned egg-cup. Leave the sweets in a cool place to dry, then add a little melted chocolate to the top of each one.

Toffee

Age range
Ten upwards.

Group size
Small groups.

What you need
100g demerara sugar,
100g butter or margarine,
2 tablespoons golden syrup,
1 small tin condensed milk.

What to do

Grease a shallow (preferably square) cake tin. Put all the ingredients into a large saucepan and bring them slowly to the boil, stirring all the time with a wooden spoon. Boil the mixture for five minutes and then begin to test the toffee. Dip the wooden spoon into the mixture and let some of the toffee drip into a bowl of cold water. When it immediately sets hard the toffee is ready. If you use a thermometer it should register 268°F.

Take the pan off the heat at once and pour the mixture into the greased tin. When it starts to set mark it in squares with a knife. Leave it to cool and set completely, then break it into squares.

Fudge

Age range
Ten upwards.

Group size
Small groups.

What you need
400g soft brown sugar,
50g butter or margarine,
½pt milk,
vanilla essence.

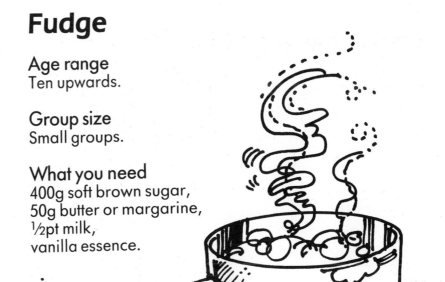

What to do

Grease a rectangular tin (about 25cm by 15cm). Put the sugar, butter and milk into a large saucepan and heat them slowly until the sugar has dissolved, then turn the heat up and bring the mixture to the boil. Allow it to boil for 15 minutes. Then, using a spoon, drip some of the mixture into a bowl of cold water. When the mixture is rubbed between your fingers it should form a soft ball. Keep boiling and testing until you have reached this stage or 235°F on a thermometer. Dip a skewer into a bottle of vanilla essence and add a few drops. Take the saucepan off the stove and beat the mixture with a wooden spoon until it becomes thick and fudgey, then pour it into the prepared tin and leave it to set.

Party hats and masks

No party is complete without party hats. Here are a few ideas for the children to make their own individual and unique designs.

Christmas pudding

Age range
Eight upwards.

Group size
Individuals.

What you need
A tape measure,
a pair of compasses,
card, paints,
adhesive,
kitchen foil,
a sprig of holly.

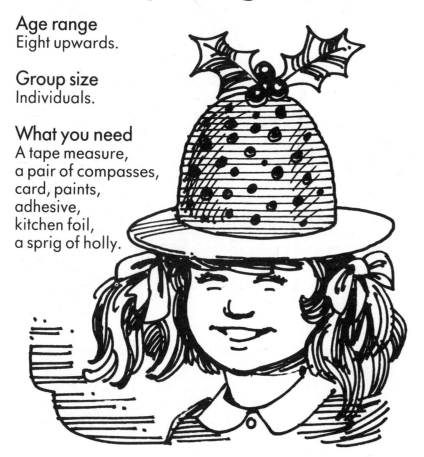

What to do
Measure the child's head, then use a pair of compasses to draw a circle with the same circumference on card. Draw a second circle about 8cm outside the first. Cut out the brim and cover it with kitchen foil to represent a plate (see figure 1).

Figure 1

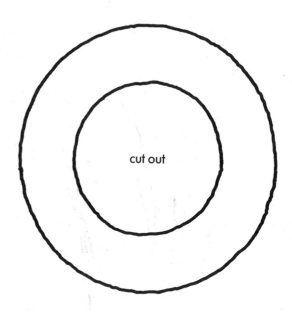

cut out

Draw a Christmas pudding shape on card, wide enough to fit round the front of the head from ear to ear and with a straight lower edge. Cut out the shape adding a 2cm tab to the straight edge.

Paint the pudding dark brown and add lots of black dots for currants.

Cut into the tab at 1cm intervals, fold it back and use it to glue the pudding on to the plate close to the inside edge.

Finally, glue a sprig of holly to the top.

Holly wreath

Age range
Eight upwards.

Group size
Individuals.

What you need
Wire,
wire cutters,
sticky tape,
metallic
crêpe paper,
florists' wire,
adhesive,
beads.

What to do
Cut and bend a length of wire to fit round the head, overlapping and joining the ends with sticky tape.

To make holly leaves, cut 5 cm squares of metallic crêpe paper, sandwich a length of florists' wire between two squares and glue them together. Cut out a holly leaf shape (see figure 1).

Figure 1

Wind the holly leaves on to the head wire, threading on beads at intervals for berries.

Angel

Age range
Eight upwards.

Group size
Individuals.

What you need
Wire,
wire cutters,
tinsel,
a plastic
hair-band,
sticky tape,
paper.

What to do
Bend a length of wire into a halo shape with a stem, and wind the end of the stem securely round a hair-band. Cover the cut end of the wire with sticky tape and bind the halo with tinsel. Cut out a pair of wings from a piece of folded paper, and secure them to the sides of the hair-band with tape.

79

Cracker hat

Age range
Five upwards.

Group size
Individuals.

What you need
A large cracker,
scissors,
a plastic
hair-band,
adhesive.

What to do
Cut a cracker in half and stick one section to either side
of a hair-band.

A Father Christmas mask

Age range
Ten upwards.

Group size
Individuals.

What you need
Red card,
strips of white
paper about 2cm wide,
knife,
adhesive tape,
white glue.

What to do
Cut a piece of card about 45cm wide according to the
size of the child's head. Bend it into a cone shape, put it
over his head and mark the eyes and mouth. Lay it flat
again and cut out the features, then bend it back into a
cone shape and fix it with tape. Cut the strips of white
paper to about 7cm long, and curl them along the blade
of a pair of scissors.

Fold a piece of white paper in half and cut a triangular shape (see figure 1).

Figure 1

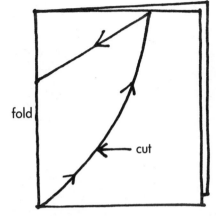

fold

cut

Open this out, stick on the curls of paper to form the beard, and stick the beard on the cone just below the mouth.

Similarly cut a moustache shape and use more curls (see figure 2). Stick the moustache in place.

Figure 2

fold

cut

Cut out a small triangle for the nose, stick on eyebrows and outline the eyes in white. Add more curls around the face for hair. Cut a circle of thin card for a hat brim and a circle for a pompon to complete the hat.

Tissue-paper masks

Age range
Eight upwards.

Group size
Individuals.

What you need
White tissue-paper, brown sticky tape (the sort that needs moistening), a piece of dampened foam sponge, string or wool.

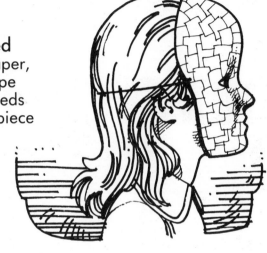

What to do
Place a sheet of tissue over the face and secure it behind the head with a short strip of tape. Make two air-holes by the nostrils.

Dampen small strips of tape – no more than 3cm long – and stick them on the tissue moulding round the face. Make sure the ends are stuck down well, and only use small pieces around the eyes and mouth. Leave the nostril area until the very last moment.

Take the mask off the face by tearing the tape from behind the head. The mask will show a great deal of detail from the model's face. When it is properly dry and hardened it can be carefully painted, and string or wool added to create the character. Make sure the paint is not too wet or the mask will sag.

Pantomimes and plays

Three things are required at Christmas time:
Plum pudding, beef and pantomime.
Folks could resist the former two;
Without the latter none could do.

Old pantomime bill.

Pantomime is a strangely British tradition which must seem very confusing to those coming across it for the first time. An older female part is always played by a man, a young man played by a girl and human beings cavort around as the front and hind parts of animals!

Pantomime is traditionally considered a children's entertainment, but many commercial productions these days are well above their heads and often sprinkled with adult jokes, mercifully incomprehensible to the innocent young.

Children would enjoy staging their own simplified version as a class project, in different forms according to their age and ability.

It might be possible to choose a pantomime being produced locally. Perhaps a trip around the theatre, with a closer look at costumes, lighting and the stage itself could be arranged. The project could end with a trip to the performance itself – but not until *after* the children's production.

If that is not possible – and this may be preferable anyway in terms of the children's own work – read a selection of the traditional fairy tales often used for pantomime: 'Aladdin', 'Dick Whittington', 'The Tinder Box', 'Snow White', 'Cinderella' and 'Puss in Boots' are all old favourites.

If the class includes children from different ethnic origins, remember the benefits of investigating the backgrounds of stories like 'Aladdin', with the help of their parents, community leaders, etc. Studies of life-style, food and customs would greatly enrich such a project.

Panto stories

Age range
Eight upwards.

Group size
Any size.

What you need
No special requirements.

What to do
Get the groups to think up as many pantomime stories as they can, based on traditional fairy stories, and discuss them. Try to make a list of the characters and features which usually appear in them. It might look like this:

Principal boy (played by a girl)

Heroine

Dame (played by a man – quite often this character is the mother of the principal boy)

Villain/demon king

Good fairy

Animal (innocent, clever – or both)

Chorus line (villagers, etc)

Song sheets (for audience to use when joining in simple, repetitive songs)

Audience participation (along the lines of 'It's behind you', 'Oh yes he did! Oh no he didn't!')

Singing, dancing and simple colourful scenery

Bright medieval type costume

Follow-up
Ask the children to work out a pantomime from a story that has not been used before. It could involve individual or group work, and could provide the basis of a class performance.

Happy ever after?

Age range
Six upwards.

Group size
Whole class.

What you need
Tape-recorder,
photocopy pages 112–119.

What to do
Discuss with the class the value of happy endings in a pantomime. What if Cinderella had been out when the prince called with the shoe? Suppose Aladdin never managed to get the lamp back, or Dick Whittington's cat had made a mistake in foiling his enemies. What would be the ending then? Try reading one of the fairy stories and stop before the end. Ask the children to complete the story on tape or paper.

Pantomime tape

Age range
Five upwards.

Group size
Any size.

What you need
Tape-recorder.

What to do
Either tell one of the familiar stories first or, with older children, work out your own. Tape-record the group working out or telling their story and play it back to them. Help them to work out a clear and simple version with different children telling different parts or speaking the parts of different characters. It might help to transcribe some of the original taping for them to read.

This could be developed into a simple performance with mime, dance and paintings for scenery, etc. Either use recorded items of appropriate music or get the children to make their own.

Designing costumes

Age range
Six upwards.

Group size
About six children.

What you need
Pencils,
thin card
(the sides of
a cereal box
would do),
felt-tipped pens,
scissors,
white glue,
scraps of
different fabrics,
wool,
sequins.

What to do
Discuss with the children what kinds of costume their characters would need. What kinds of fabric would they be made from? How would they be decorated? Would the character need more than one set of clothes (as in rags to riches stories)?

Get the group to choose one major character each. Ask them to draw the outline of the person on the card; point out how tall it needs to be and remind the children that thin arms and legs are liable to fall off when cut out!

'Dress' the character with appropriate materials, and use felt-tipped pens for the features and wool for hair.

Older children might like to do the back of the character as well and make a cardboard prop so that it can stand up.

This could be adapted to 'hinged' clothes, which could be hooked on to the cut-out figure with tabs, thus making it possible to try out different costumes.

Bottle characters

Age range
Seven upwards.

Group size
About six children.

What you need
A plastic bottle
(washing-up liquid
containers are fine),
paste,
white kitchen paper,
white card,
felt-tipped pens,
scissors,
scraps of fabric and fur,
wool,
white glue,
art straws.

Figure 1

What to do
Get the groups to cover the bottle with strips of white
paper, making sure all the ends are stuck down well. Cut
two small armholes and thread an art straw through to
form arms. Cut out a circle of white card for the head,
leaving a strip at the bottom (see figure 1).

Colour the head and add features using felt-tipped
pens and wool for hair. Place the strip in the neck of the
bottle, then stick on suitable material for the character's
costume, remembering to include sleeves. Add details
like a belt, hat, jewellery, crowns, etc.

These designs could be used, in association with kindly
volunteers, as a basis for costumes for the performance,
if one is to be staged.

Paper-bag masks

Age range
Eight upwards.

Group size
Individuals.

What you need
A large paper sack,
scissors,
paints,
materials for decoration.

What to do
This is a simple way to make an all-in-one animal
costume and mask. Mark and cut the position of the eyes,
nose and mouth at the top of the sealed end of the sack.
Do this by holding the bag in front of the child's face.
About 30cm from the top, cut two holes at the sides for the
armholes. Use paints to create the character on both
sides. Feathers, raffia, pipe-cleaners, string, etc, can be
used for additional decoration. Add a tail if required.

Pantomime puppets

Age range
Seven upwards.

Group size
Individuals.

What you need
Paper,
card,
coloured pencils or pens,
scissors,
a knitting needle,
a darning needle,
strong thread,
thin cord,
a bead,
brass paper-fasteners.

What to do
Let the children draw their own figures on a folded sheet of paper. Draw half the body and the limbs along the fold, then cut the figure out, so that when the paper is unfolded the figure will be symmetrical.

Using the paper pieces as a pattern, trace the figure on to card. The children can colour and decorate the figures before cutting them out.

Using a knitting needle, pierce the holes needed for the paper-fasteners. These holes should be large enough to allow the fasteners to move around freely.

Use a darning needle to make smaller holes for attaching strong thread to the limbs. Do not make these holes too close to the edge of the card or it will tear. Then join the limbs together in pairs.

Lay out the joined limbs across the body and push the paper-fasteners through the corresponding holes from the front, and fasten them.

Join the threads that move the limbs to a length of fine cord and add a small bead at the end for decoration. Pull the cord to make the figure move.

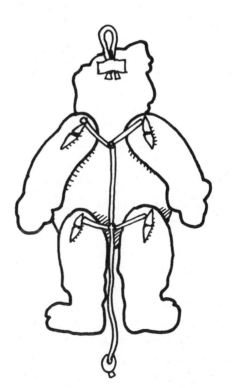

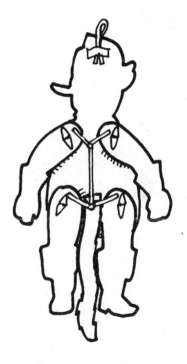

A simple rod puppet

Age range
Six upwards with some help.

Group size
Small groups.

What you need
An old sock
or one leg of
a pair of tights,
a stick,
some thread,
stuffing,
wool,
a piece of material
and odd scraps
for decoration.

Stuff the end of a sock or the leg of a pair of tights to make a ball shape. Then push the stick inside and tie with the thread to hold the stick in place. Use wool for hair and scraps of material to make the features. Run a thread along one side of the piece of material and pull it up to make the body. Wrap it around the stick and glue it into place.

Figure 1   Figure 2

What to do
A range of these could be made to include all the principals of the cast, and the story acted out using the puppets as performers. They could also be used in conjunction with the children's tape (see 'Pantomime tape' on page 85).

Papier mâché puppets

Age range
Ten upwards.

Group size
Individuals.

What you need
Newspaper,
kitchen paper,
paste,
small cardboard tube,
scissors,
paper,
material,
paints,
wool.

What to do
Each child roughly pleats a piece of newspaper, folds it in two, twists the ends together and pushes them into the small cardboard tube (see figure 1).

Figure 1

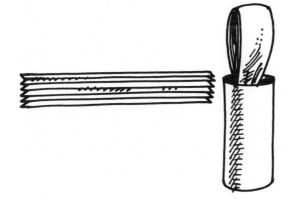

Get them to tear up some small pieces of newspaper and paste them on to the ball of paper, covering it completely and making sure the ends are stuck down well. Join the newspaper to the cardboard tube with a 'collar' of small pieces (see figure 2).

Figure 2

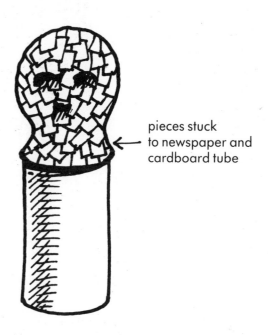

pieces stuck to newspaper and cardboard tube

Repeat this for a few layers and then begin to build up the features. Gently push fingers into the head for the eye sockets and pinch up sections to form the nose and chin. Build these up with tiny pieces of paper and glue. Finish off with a layer of white kitchen paper and allow the whole thing to dry thoroughly.

Put the tube in a container to hold it steady while it is painted. Stick wool on for hair, and allow it to dry. Carefully cut the cardboard tube to just below the newspaper collar. Gently tear out enough of the original ball of newspaper to leave room for fingers in the head.

Make a pattern for the body by spreading your hand on a piece of paper and drawing round it (see figure 3).

Figure 3

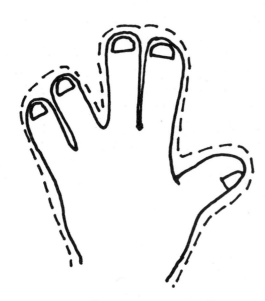

Cut the shape out, allowing an extra 1cm, and pin it on to a double thickness of material. Allow enough material to put it on to the collar. Sew or stick the material together, then stick it on to the head and decorate as required for the character.

Posters and programmes

Age range
Ten upwards.

Group size
Individuals,
but could also be worked
as a small group
project.

What you need
Wooden frame or strong picture frame, fine but strong material such as cotton, organdie, silk, net curtain material, staples or drawing-pins, brown tape, sponge, tracing paper or kitchen paper, dense felt tipped pens, poster paint, fabric paint or printing ink (oil- or water-based).

What to do

Young children can draw their own posters and programmes which can be photocopied. The originals should be drawn using dense felt-tipped pens for maximum effect.

Older children might like to try this more sophisticated but simple method of silk screen printing.

The fine material should be stretched over the frame and pinned or stapled tightly in position. Tape all around the sides of the frame and make a well on one side. Place the printing paper on a hard flat base and place the stencil on top. This can be made from torn or cut shapes in tracing paper or kitchen paper which has been cut to the outside size of the screen.

The ink should be fairly thin and poured into the well. Pull it with a squeegee over the surface of the screen. This forces the ink through the screen and that makes the stencil stick to it. The parts of the printing paper not protected by the stencil will be printed. This technique can be adapted to all kinds of design.

Reproducible Material

Merry Christmas

OICHE NODLAIG MHAITH
(Irish)

کرسمس مبارک
(Urdu)

Vesele Vanoch
(Czech)

Fröhliche Weihnachten
(German)

क्रिस्मस मुबारिक हो
(Hindi)

GELUKKIG KERSTFEEST
(Dutch)

GLAD JUL
(Swedish)

Hauskaa Joulua
(Finnish)

ਕਾਗਮਭਮ ਸਘਾਭ੍ਰ ਹੋੲ
(Punjabi)

Merry Christmas

Buone Feste Natalizie
(Italian)

Gledig Jul
(Norwegian)

Nadolig Llawen
(Welsh)

聖旦 旦快樂
(Chinese)

Joyeux Noël
(French)

Bozego Narodzenia
(Polish)

SARBATORI FERICITE
(Rumanian)

FELIZ NAVIDAD
(Spanish)

The presents I would like....

1
2
3
4
5
6
7
8
9
10

Name:

Class:

Good things I have done.

Bathed the rabbit.
Hid Sarah's lunchbox.

Not-so-good things I have done.

You have 50p to choose from these snacks

chocolate biscuits **5p**

6p glass lemonade

LEMONADE

10p a bag sticky sweets

mince pies **4p** each

cheese **2p** a cube

apples **2p** each

oranges **8p** each

carrots **3p** each

I would choose

Price

_____ _____

_____ _____

_____ _____

_____ _____

_____ _____

_____ _____

_____

50p
_____

I chose these things because

_____

_____

_____

Dear Father Christmas
I would like _____

_____

_____

_____

_____

_____

please send _____
to _____
because _____

_____

love from _____

Flying reindeer, see page 24

Help Santa deliver the presents, see page 25

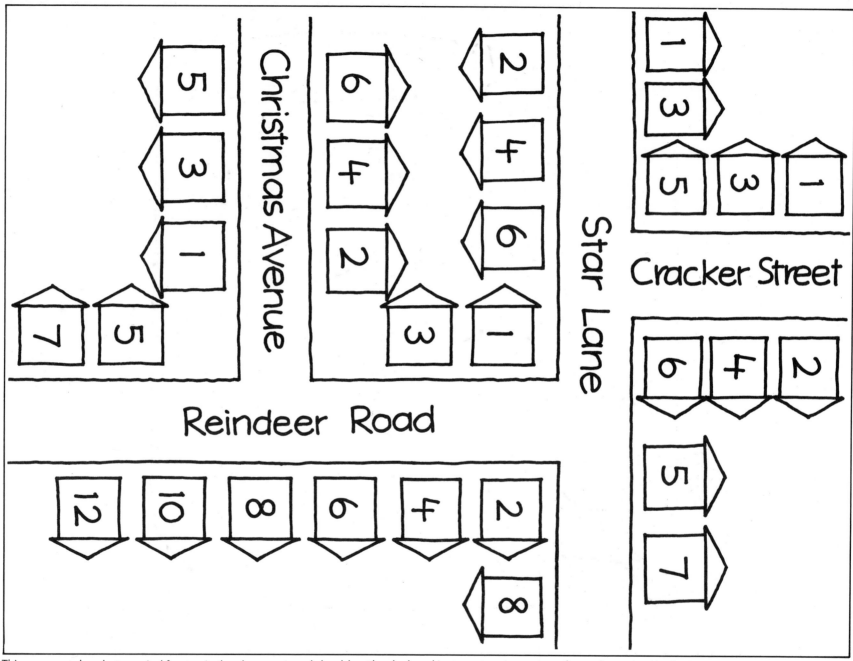

House number:

Street:

Design your own stamps.

Candle burning, see page 52

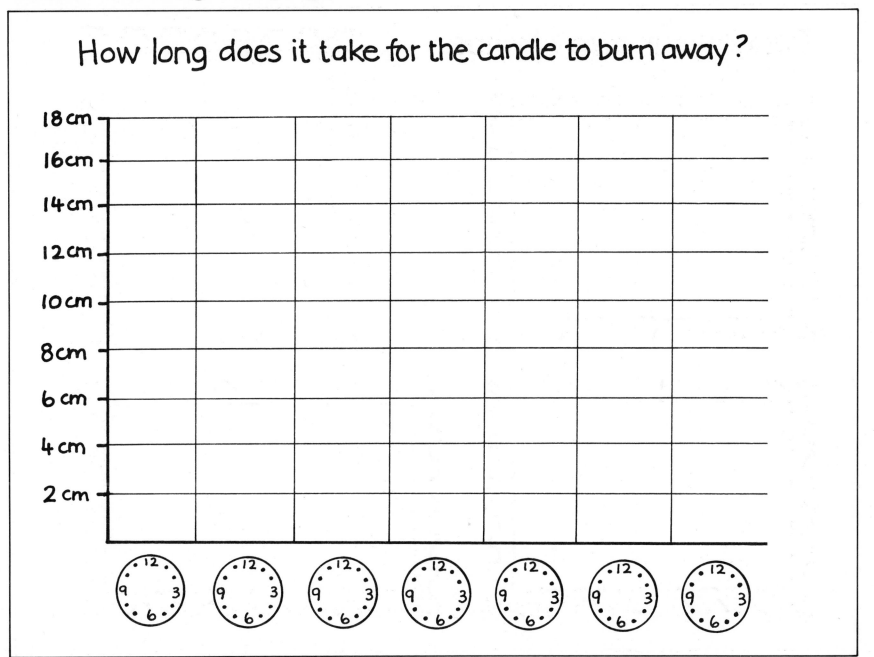

How long does it take for the candle to burn away?

18 cm
16 cm
14 cm
12 cm
10 cm
8 cm
6 cm
4 cm
2 cm

While the candle was burning I noticed

1   ( )
2   ( )
3   ( )
4   ( )
5   ( )
6   ( )
7   ( )
8   ( )
9   ( )
10   ( )

When it went out I noticed _____ ( )
_____ ( )
_____ ( )

Write your score in the brackets
My total was ☐

Before it was lit I noticed

1   ( )

2   ( )

3   ( )

4   ( )

5   ( )

6   ( )

7   ( )

8   ( )

9   ( )

10   ( )

Write your scores in the brackets.

My total was [ ]

Sandwich graph, see page 72

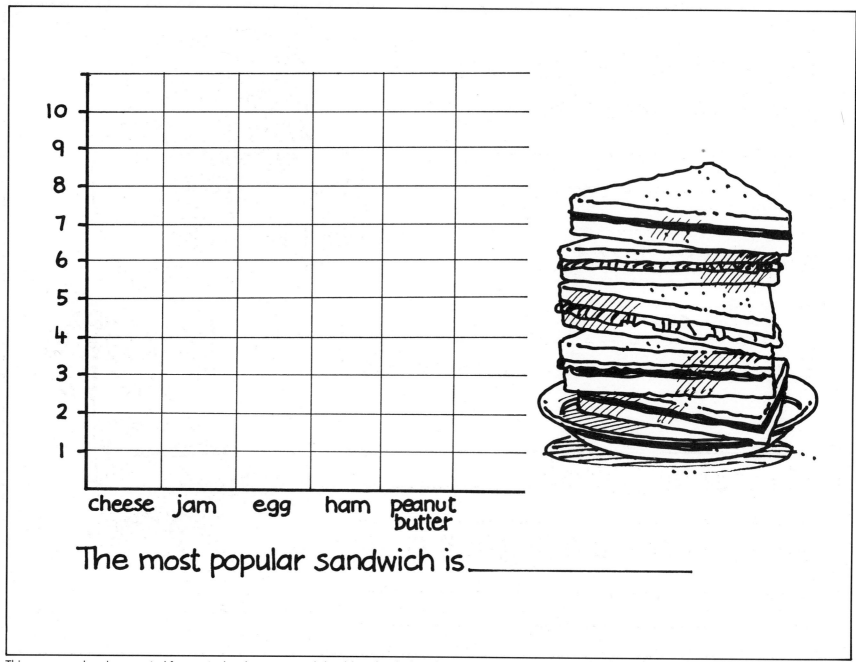

The most popular sandwich is_____

When she was a little girl
my mum liked playing____

_____

_____

_____

My granny liked____

_____

_____

When he was a boy my dad liked

_____

_____

My grandad liked ____

_____

My favourite party game is ____

_____

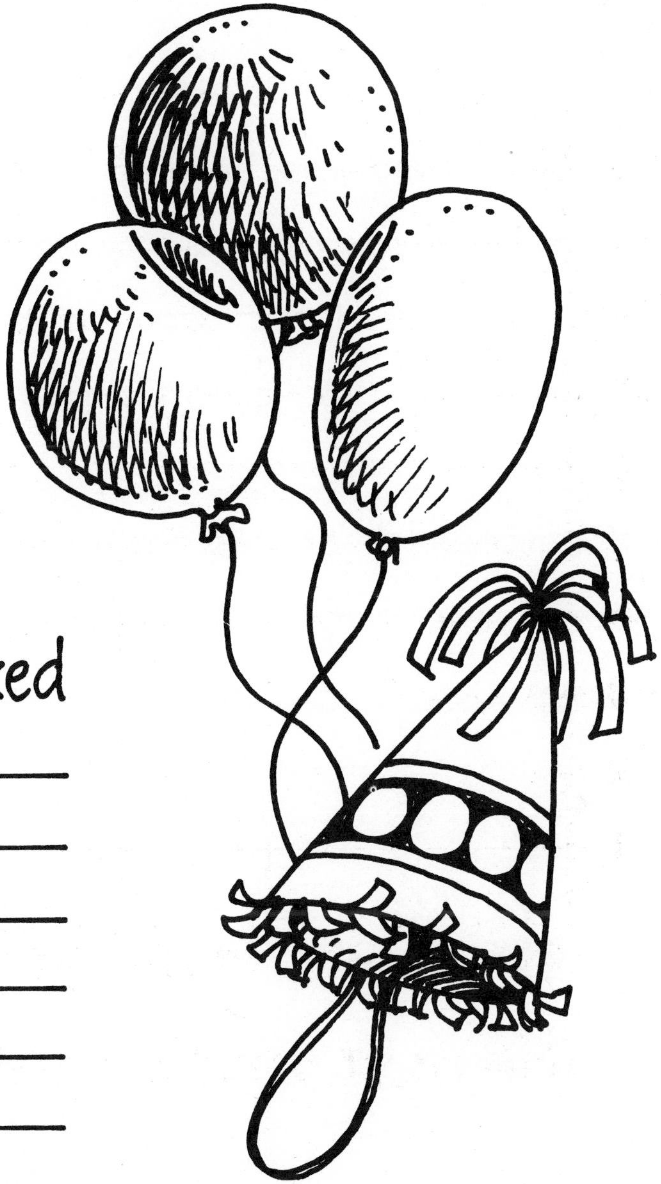

Finish the story.

Cinderella

Cinderella had two sisters. They treated her like a servant and told her she could not go to the ball at the palace. Cinderella's fairy-godmother turned her rags into a ball gown and a pumpkin into a coach. So Cinderella went to the ball and met the prince. But she had to leave at midnight before her gown turned back to rags. As she hurried away . . .

Finish the story.

Puss-in-Boots

A miller died and left his youngest son a cat. The cat said to the son that in return for a pair of boots and a sack, he would catch their food. The son agreed to this. The cat had a plan to make the son seem rich, so that he could marry the princess . . .

Finish the story.

Jack and the Beanstalk

Jack was very poor. He took a cow to the market and swapped it for some magic beans. He planted them and after a while a giant beanstalk grew all the way up to the clouds. Jack climbed the beanstalk and found a giant's castle. As he went inside he heard . . .

Happy ever after?, see page 85

Finish the story.

Aladdin

Aladdin and his mother were poor. One day his
uncle came to visit them and promised to make
them both rich if Aladdin did a small task for him.
The man was not really his uncle but a magician.
He took Aladdin up the mountains to a cave and
told him to get the old lamp that was inside.
Aladdin found the lamp which he rubbed and a
genie appeared . . .

Help Cinderella find her lost shoe

The game is for two to four players.
Each player needs two counters of the same colour. You also need a die.

How to play

Each player puts one counter at a Start and the second on the adjoining line of spaces (as shown on the board).

A six must be thrown to move each counter. The player whose counters arrive at the centre circle at the same time is the winner.

Moves can be made in both directions. The throws can be split: for example, if a four is thrown, one counter can be moved one space and the other three spaces.

If a player lands on a pumpkin, he has to go back to the beginning of that line (the second counter can stay where it is).

If a player lands on a ragged dress, he has to go back two places.

If a player lands on a mouse, he has to miss a go.

If a player lands on a magic wand, he can tell one of the other players to go back to the beginning of both lines.

17th Edition
IEE Wiring Regulations:
Explained and Illustrated

Eighth edition

Brian Scaddan IEng, MIET

ELSEVIER

AMSTERDAM • BOSTON • HEIDELBERG • LONDON
NEW YORK • OXFORD • PARIS • SAN DIEGO
SAN FRANCISCO • SINGAPORE • SYDNEY • TOKYO
Newnes is an imprint of Elsevier

Newnes

Newnes is an imprint of Elsevier
Linacre House, Jordan Hill, Oxford OX2 8DP, UK
30 Corporate Drive, Suite 400, Burlington, MA 01803, USA

First published 1989
Second edition 1991
Third edition 1996
Fourth edition 1998
Fifth edition 2001
Sixth edition 2002
Reprinted 2002, 2003, 2004
Seventh edition 2005
Eighth edition 2008

British Library Cataloguing in Publication Data
Scaddan, Brian
   17th edition IEE wiring regulations : explained and illustrated. – 8th ed.
   1. Electric wiring, Interior – Safety regulations – Great Britain 2. Electric wiring,
   Interior – Handbooks, manuals, etc.
   I. Title   II. Scaddan, Brain. 16th edition IEE wiring regulations   III. Institution
   of Electrical Engineers   IV. Seventeenth edition IEE wiring regulations
   621.3'1924'0941

Library of Congress Control Number: 2008927641

ISBN: 978-0-7506-8720-1

For information on all Newnes publications
visit our website at www.elsevierdirect.com

Typeset by Charon Tec Ltd., A Macmillan Company. (www.macmillansolutions.com)

Printed and bound in Slovenia

08 09 10 11   11 10 9 8 7 6 5 4 3 2 1

Contents

Preface

As a result of many years developing and teaching courses devoted to compliance with the IEE Wiring Regulations, it has become apparent to me that many operatives and personnel in the electrical contracting industry have forgotten the basic principles and concepts upon which electric power supply and its use are based. As a result of this, misconceived ideas and much confusion have arisen over the interpretation of the Regulations.

It is the intention of this book to dispel such misconceptions and to educate and where necessary refresh the memory of the reader. In this respect, emphasis has been placed on those areas where most confusion arises, namely earthing and bonding, protection, and circuit design.

The current seventeenth edition of the IEE Wiring Regulations, also known as BS 7671, to which this book conforms, was published in January 2008. This book is *not* a guide to the Regulations or a replacement for them; nor does it seek to interpret them Regulation by Regulation. It should, in fact, be read in conjunction with them; to help the reader, each chapter cites the relevant Regulation numbers for cross-reference.

It is hoped that the book will be found particularly useful by college students, electricians and technicians, and also by managers of smaller electrical contracting firms that do not normally employ engineers or designers. It should also be a useful addition to the library of those studying for the C&G 2382 series qualifications.

Brian Scaddan, April 2008

Material on Part P in Chapter 1 is taken from *Building Regulations Approved Document P: Electrical Safety – Dwellings*, P1 Design and installation of electrical installations (The Stationery Office, 2006) ISBN 9780117036536. © Crown copyright material is reproduced with the permission of the Controller of HMSO and Queen's Printer for Scotland.

Acknowledgements

I would like to thank Paul Clifford for his thorough technical proof reading.

Introduction

It was once said, by whom I have no idea, that 'rules and regulations are for the guidance of wise men and the blind obedience of fools'. This is certainly true in the case of the IEE Wiring (BS 7671) Regulations. They are not statutory rules, but recommendations for the safe selection and erection of wiring installations. Earlier editions were treated as an 'electrician's Bible': the Regulations now take the form primarily of a design document.

The IEE Wiring Regulations are divided into seven parts. These follow a logical pattern from the basic requirements to inspection and testing of an installation and finally to the requirements for special locations:

Part 1 indicates the range and type of installations covered by the Regulations, what they are intended for, and the basic requirements for safety.

Part 2 is devoted to the definitions of the terms used throughout the Regulations.

Part 3 details the general information needed and the fundamental principles to be adopted before any design work can usefully proceed.

Part 4 informs the designer of the different methods available for protection against electric shock, overcurrent, etc., and how to apply those methods.

Part 5 enables the correct type of equipment, cable, accessory, etc. to be selected and erected in accordance with the requirements of Parts 1–4.

Part 6 provides details of the relevant tests to be performed on a completed installation before it is energized.

Part 7 deals with particular requirements for special installations and locations such as bathrooms, swimming pools, construction sites, etc.

Appendices 1–15 provide tabulated and other background information required by the designer/installer/tester.

It must be remembered that the Regulations are not a collection of unrelated statements each to be interpreted in isolation; there are many cross-references throughout which may render such an interpretation valueless.

In using the Regulations I have found the index an invaluable starting place when seeking information. However, one may have to try different combinations of wording in order to locate a particular item. For example, determining how often an RCD should be tested via its test button could prove difficult since no reference is made under 'Residual current devices' or 'Testing'; however, 'Periodic testing' leads to Regulation 514.12, and the information in question is found in 514.12.2. In the index, this Regulation is referred under 'Notices'.

CHAPTER 1

Fundamental Requirements for Safety

IEE WIRING REGULATIONS (IEE REGULATIONS PART 1 AND CHAPTER 13)

It does not require a degree in electrical engineering to realize that electricity at *low* voltage can, if uncontrolled, present a serious threat of injury to persons or livestock, or damage to property by fire.

Clearly the type and arrangement of the equipment used, together with the quality of workmanship provided, will go a long way to minimizing danger. The following is a list of basic requirements:

1. Use good workmanship.
2. Use approved materials and equipment.
3. Ensure that the correct type, size and current-carrying capacity of cables are chosen.
4. Ensure that equipment is suitable for the maximum power demanded of it.
5. Make sure that conductors are insulated, and sheathed or protected if necessary, or are placed in a position to prevent danger.
6. Joints and connections should be properly constructed to be mechanically and electrically sound.
7. Always provide overcurrent protection for every circuit in an installation (the protection for the whole installation is usually provided by the Distribution Network Operator

[DNO]), and ensure that protective devices are suitably chosen for their location and the duty they have to perform.

8. Where there is a chance of metalwork becoming live owing to a fault, it should be earthed, and the circuit concerned should be protected by an overcurrent device or a residual current device (RCD).

9. Ensure that all necessary bonding of services is carried out.

10. Do not place a fuse, a switch or a circuit breaker, unless it is a linked switch or circuit breaker, in an earthed neutral conductor. The linked type must be arranged to break all the line conductors.

11. All single-pole switches must be wired in the line conductor only.

12. A readily accessible and effective means of isolation must be provided, so that all voltage may be cut off from an installation or any of its circuits.

13. All motors must have a readily accessible means of disconnection.

14. Ensure that any item of equipment which may normally need operating or attending by persons is accessible and easily operated.

15. Any equipment required to be installed in a situation exposed to weather or corrosion, or in explosive or volatile environments, should be of the correct type for such adverse conditions.

16. Before adding to or altering an installation, ensure that such work will not impair any part of the existing installation and that the existing is in a safe condition to accommodate the addition.

17. After completion of an installation or an alteration to an installation, the work must be inspected and tested to ensure, as far as reasonably practicable, that the fundamental requirements for safety have been met.

These requirements form the basis of the IEE Regulations.

It is interesting to note that, whilst the Wiring Regulations are not statutory, they may be used to claim compliance with Statutory Regulations such as the Electricity at Work Regulations, the Health and Safety at Work Act and Part 'P' of the Building Regulations. In fact, the Health and Safety Executive produces guidance notes for installations in such places as schools and construction sites. The contents of these documents reinforce and extend the requirements of the IEE Regulations. Extracts from the Health and Safety at Work Act, the Electricity at Work Regulations and Part 'P' of the Building Regulations are reproduced below.

THE HEALTH AND SAFETY AT WORK ACT 1974

Duties of employers

Employers must safeguard, as far as is reasonably practicable, the health, safety and welfare of all the people who work for them. This applies in particular to the provision and maintenance of safe plant and systems of work, and covers all machinery, equipment and appliances used.

Some examples of the matters which many employers need to consider are:

1. Is all plant up to the necessary standards with respect to safety and risk to health?
2. When new plant is installed, is latest good practice taken into account?
3. Are systems of work safe? Thorough checks of all operations, especially those operations carried out infrequently, will ensure that danger of injury or to health is minimized. This may require special safety systems, such as 'permits to work'.

4. Is the work environment regularly monitored to ensure that, where known toxic contaminants are present, protection conforms to current hygiene standards?
5. Is monitoring also carried out to check the adequacy of control measures?
6. Is safety equipment regularly inspected? All equipment and appliances for safety and health, such as personal protective equipment, dust and fume extraction, guards, safe access arrangement, monitoring and testing devices, need regular inspection (Section 2(1) and 2(2) of the Act).

No charge may be levied on any employee for anything done or provided to meet any specific requirement for health and safety at work (Section 9).

Risks to health from the use, storage, or transport of 'articles' and 'substances' must be minimized. The term *substance* is defined as 'any natural or artificial substance whether in solid or liquid form or in the form of gas or vapour' (Section 53(1)).

To meet these aims, all reasonably practicable precautions must be taken in the handling of any substance likely to cause a risk to health. Expert advice can be sought on the correct labelling of substances, and the suitability of containers and handling devices. All storage and transport arrangements should be kept under review.

Safety information and training

It is now the duty of employers to provide any necessary information and training in safe practices, including information on legal requirements.

Duties to others

Employers must also have regard for the health and safety of the self-employed or contractors' employees who may be working close to their own employees, and for the health and safety of the public who may be affected by their firm's activities.

Similar responsibilities apply to self-employed persons, manufacturers and suppliers.

Duties of employees

Employees have a duty under the Act to take reasonable care to avoid injury to themselves or to others by their work activities, and to cooperate with employers and others in meeting statutory requirements. The Act also requires employees not to interfere with or misuse anything provided to protect their health, safety or welfare in compliance with the Act.

THE ELECTRICITY AT WORK REGULATIONS 1989

Persons on whom duties are imposed by these Regulations

1. Except where otherwise expressly provided in these Regulations, it shall be the duty of every:
   a. employer and self-employed person to comply with the provisions of these Regulations in so far as they relate to matters which are within his control; and
   b. manager of a mine or quarry (within in either case the meaning of Section 180 of the Mines and Quarries Act 1954) to ensure that all requirements or prohibitions imposed by or under these Regulations are complied with in so far as they relate to the mine or quarry or part of a quarry of which he is the manager and to matters which are within his control.

2. It shall be the duty of every employee while at work:
   a. to cooperate with his employer in so far as is necessary to enable any duty placed on that employer by the provisions of these Regulations to be complied with; and
   b. to comply with the provisions of these Regulations in so far as they relate to matters which are within his control.

Employer

1. For the purposes of the Regulations, an employer is any person or body who (a) employs one or more individuals under a contract of employment or apprenticeship; or (b) provides training under the schemes to which the HSW Act applies through the Health and Safety (Training for Employment) Regulations 1988 (Statutory Instrument No. 1988/1222).

Self-employed

2. A self-employed person is an individual who works for gain or reward otherwise than under a contract of employment whether or not he employs others.

Employee

3. Regulation 3(2)(a) reiterates the duty placed on employees by Section 7(b) of the HSW Act.
4. Regulation 3(2)(b) places duties on employees equivalent to those placed on employers and self-employed persons where these are matters within their control. This will include those trainees who will be considered as employees under the Regulations described in paragraph 1.

5. This arrangement recognizes the level of responsibility which many employees in the electrical trades and professions are expected to take on as part of their job. The 'control' which they exercise over the electrical safety in any particular circumstances will determine to what extent they hold responsibilities under the Regulations to ensure that the Regulations are complied with.

6. A person may find himself responsible for causing danger to arise elsewhere in an electrical system, at a point beyond his own installation. This situation may arise, for example, due to unauthorized or unscheduled back feeding from his installation onto the system, or to raising the fault power level on the system above rated and agreed maximum levels due to connecting extra generation capacity, etc. Because such circumstances are 'within his control', the effect of Regulation 3 is to bring responsibilities for compliance with the rest of the regulations to that person, thus making him a duty holder.

Absolute/reasonably practicable

7. Duties in some of the Regulations are subject to the qualifying term 'reasonably practicable'. Where qualifying terms are absent the requirement in the Regulation is said to be absolute. The meaning of reasonably practicable has been well established in law. The interpretations below are given only as a guide to duty holders.

Absolute

8. If the requirement in a Regulation is 'absolute', for example if the requirement is not qualified by the words 'so far as is reasonably practicable', the requirement must be met

regardless of cost or any other consideration. Certain of the regulations making such absolute requirements are subject to the Defence provision of Regulation 29.

Reasonably practicable

9. Someone who is required to do something 'so far as is reasonably practicable' must assess, on the one hand, the magnitude of the risks of a particular work activity or environment and, on the other hand, the costs in terms of the physical difficulty, time, trouble and expense which would be involved in taking steps to eliminate or minimize those risks. If, for example, the risks to health and safety of a particular work process are very low, and the cost or technical difficulties of taking certain steps to prevent those risks are very high, it might not be reasonably practicable to take those steps. The greater the degree of risk, the less weight that can be given to the cost of measures needed to prevent that risk.

10. In the context of the Regulations, where the risk is very often that of death, for example from electrocution, and where the nature of the precautions which can be taken are so often very simple and cheap, e.g. insulation, the level of duty to prevent that danger approaches that of an absolute duty.

11. The comparison does not include the financial standing of the duty holder. Furthermore, where someone is prosecuted for failing to comply with a duty 'so far as is reasonably practicable', it would be for the accused to show the court that it was not reasonably practicable for him to do more than he had in fact done to comply with the duty (Section 40 of the HSW Act).

AN EXTRACT FROM THE BUILDING REGULATIONS APPROVED DOCUMENT 'P'

Certification of notifiable work

a. Where the installer is registered with a Part P competent person self-certification scheme

1.18 Installers registered with a Part P competent person self-certification scheme are qualified to complete BS 7671 installation certificates and should do so in respect of every job they undertake. A copy of the certificate should always be given to the person ordering the electrical installation work.

1.19 Where Installers are registered with a Part P competent person self-certification scheme, a Building Regulations compliance certificate must be issued to the occupant either by the installer or the installer's registration body within 30 days of the work being completed. The relevant building control body should also receive a copy of the information on the certificate within 30 days.

1.20 The Regulations call for the Building Regulations compliance certificate to be issued to the occupier. However, in the case of rented properties, the certificate may be sent to the person ordering the work with a copy sent also to the occupant.

b. Where the installer is *not* registered with a Part P competent person self-certification scheme but qualified to complete BS 7671 installation certificates

1.21 Where notifiable electrical installer work is carried out by a person not registered with a Part P competent person self-certification the work should be notified to a building control body (the local authority or an approved inspector) before work starts. Where the work is necessary because of an emergency the building control body should be notified as soon as possible. The building control body becomes responsible for making sure the work is safe and complies with all relevant requirements of the Building Regulations.

1.22 Where installers are qualified to carry out inspection and testing and completing the appropriate BS 7671 installation certificate, they should do so. A copy of the certificate should then be given to the building control body. The building control body will take this certificate into account in deciding what further action (if any) needs to be taken to make sure that the work is safe and complies fully with all relevant requirements. Building control bodies may ask for evidence that installers are qualified in this case.

1.23 Where the building control body decides that the work is safe and meets all building regulation requirements it will issue a building regulation completion certificate (the local authority) on request or a final certificate (an approved inspector).

c. **Where installers are not qualified to complete BS 7671 completion certificates**

1.24 Where such installers (who may be contractors or DIYers) carry out notifiable electrical work, the building control body must be notified before the work starts. Where the work is necessary because of an emergency the building control body should be notified as soon as possible. The building control body then becomes responsible for making sure that the work is safe and complies with all relevant requirements in the Building Regulations.

1.25 The amount of inspection and testing needed is for the building control body to decide based on the nature and extent of the electrical work. For relatively simple notifiable jobs, such as adding a socket outlet to a kitchen circuit, the inspection and testing requirements will be minimal. For a house rewire, a full set of inspection and tests may need to be carried out.

1.26 The building control body may choose to carry out the inspection and testing itself, or to contract out some or all of the work to a special body which will then carry out the work on its behalf. Building control bodies will carry out the necessary inspection and testing at their expense, not at the householders' expense.

1.27 A building control body will **not** issue a BS 7671 installation certificate (as these can be issued only by those carrying out the work), but only a Building Regulations completion certificate (the local authority) or a final certificate (an approved inspector).

Third party certification

1.28 Unregistered installers should not themselves arrange for a third party to carry out final inspection and testing. The third party – not having supervised the work from the outset – would not be in a position to verify that the installation work complied fully with BS 7671:2008 requirements. An electrical installation certificate can be issued only by the installer responsible for the installation work.

1.29 A third party could only sign a BS 7671:2008 Periodic Inspection Report or similar. The Report would indicate that electrical safety tests had been carried out on the installation which met BS 7671:2008 criteria, but it could not verify that the installation complied fully with BS 7671:2008 requirements – for example, with regard to routing of hidden cables.

Part 'P'

The following material is taken from *The Building Regulations 2000 approved document P*. © Crown copyright material is reproduced with the permission of the Controller of HMSO and Queen's Printer for Scotland.

Part 'P' of the building Regulations requires that certain electrical installation work in domestic dwellings be certified and notified to the Local Authority Building Control (LABC). Failure to provide this notification may result in substantial fines.

Who am I and what do I do?

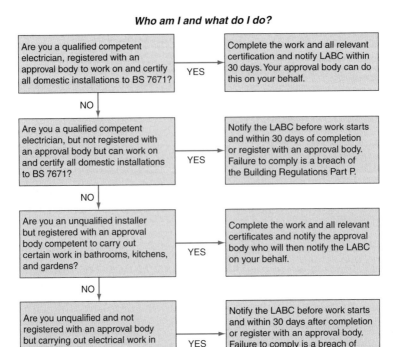

| Are you a qualified competent electrician, registered with an approval body to work on and certify all domestic installations to BS 7671? | YES | Complete the work and all relevant certification and notify LABC within 30 days. Your approval body can do this on your behalf. |

NO

| Are you a qualified competent electrician, but not registered with an approval body but can work on and certify all domestic installations to BS 7671? | YES | Notify the LABC before work starts and within 30 days of completion or register with an approval body. Failure to comply is a breach of the Building Regulations Part P. |

NO

| Are you an unqualified installer but registered with an approval body competent to carry out certain work in bathrooms, kitchens, and gardens? | YES | Complete the work and all relevant certificates and notify the approval body who will then notify the LABC on your behalf. |

NO

| Are you unqualified and not registered with an approval body but carrying out electrical work in dwellings? | YES | Notify the LABC before work starts and within 30 days after completion or register with an approval body. Failure to comply is a breach of the Building Regulations Part P. |

FIGURE 1.1

Some approval bodies offer registration for all electrical work in domestic premises; these are known as full scope schemes (FS). Other bodies offer registration for certain limited work in special locations such as kitchens, bathrooms, gardens, etc. these are known as defined scope schemes (DS).

In order to achieve and maintain competent person status, all approval bodies require an initial and thereafter annual registration fee and inspection visit.

Approval bodies (full scope FS and defined scope DS)

NICEIC	(FS) & (DS)	0870 013 0900
NAPIT	(FS) & (DS)	0870 444 1392
ELESCA	(FS) & (DS)	0870 749 0080

BSI	(FS)	01442 230 442
BRE	(FS)	0870 609 6093
CORGI	(DS)	01256 392 200
OFTEC	(DS)	0845 658 5080

Table 1.1 Examples of Work Notifiable and Not Notifiable.

Notifiable (YES) Examples of Work	Not Notifiable (NO) Location A Within Kitchens, Bath/Shower Room, Gardens, Swimming/ Paddling Pools and Hot Air Saunas	Not Applicable (N/A) Location B Outside of Location A
A complete new installation or rewire	YES	YES
Consumer unit change	YES	YES
Installing a new final circuit (e.g. for lighting, socket outlets, a shower or a cooker)	YES	YES
Fitting and connecting an electric shower to an existing wiring point	YES	N/A
Adding a socket outlet to an existing final circuit	YES	NO
Adding a lighting point to an existing final circuit	YES	NO
Adding a fused connection unit to an existing final circuit	YES	NO
Installing and fitting a storage heater including final circuit	YES	YES
Installing extra-low voltage lighting (other than pre-assembled CE marked sets)	YES	YES
Installing a new supply to a garden shed or other building	YES	N/A
Installing a socket outlet or lighting point in a garden shed or other detached outbuilding	YES	N/A
Installing a garden pond pump, including supply	YES	N/A

(*continued*)

Table 1.1 *Continued*

Notifiable (YES)	Not Notifiable (NO)	Not Applicable (N/A)
Examples of Work	**Location A** Within Kitchens, Bath/Shower Room, Gardens, Swimming/ Paddling Pools and Hot Air Saunas	**Location B** Outside of Location A
Installing an electric hot air sauna	YES	N/A
Installing a solar photovoltaic power supply	YES	YES
Installing electric ceiling or floor heating	YES	YES
Installing an electricity generator	YES	YES
Installing telephone or extra low-voltage wiring and equipment for communications, information technology, signalling, control or similar purposes	YES	NO
Installing a socket outlet or lighting point outdoors	YES	YES
Installing or upgrading main or supplementary equipotential bonding	NO	NO
Connecting a cooker to an existing connection unit	NO	NO
Replacing a damaged cable for a single circuit, on a like-for-like basis	NO	NO
Replacing a damaged accessory, such as a socket outlet	NO	NO
Replacing a lighting fitting	NO	NO
Providing mechanical protection to an existing fixed installation	NO	NO
Fitting and final connection of storage heater to an existing adjacent wiring point	NO	NO
Connecting an item of equipment to an existing adjacent connection point	NO	NO
Replacing an immersion heater	NO	NO
Installing an additional socket outlet in a motor caravan	N/A	N/A

Appendix 2 of the IEE Regulations lists all of the other Statutory Regulations and Memoranda with which electrical installations must comply.

It is interesting to note that if an installation fails to comply with Chapter 13 of the Regulations, the DNO has the right to refuse to give a supply or, in certain circumstances, to disconnect it.

While we are on the subject of DNOs, let us look at the current declared supply voltages and tolerances. In order to align with European Harmonized Standards, our historic 415 V/240 V declared supply voltages have now become 400 V/230 V. However,

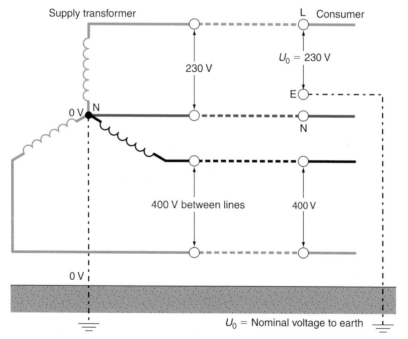

Note: The connection of the transformer star or neutral point to earth helps to maintain that point at or very near zero volts.

FIGURE 1.2 DNO Supply Voltages.

this is only a paper exercise, and it is unlikely that consumers will notice any difference for many years, if at all. Let me explain, using single phase as the example.

The supply industry declared voltage was 240 V ± 6%, giving a range between 225.6 V and 254.4 V. The new values are 230 V + 10% − 6%, giving a range between 216.2 V and 253 V. Not a lot of difference. The industry has done nothing physical to reduce voltages from 240 V to 230 V, it is just the declaration that has been altered. Hence a measurement of voltage at supply terminals will give similar readings to those we have always known. Figure 1.2 shows the UK supply system and associated declared voltages.

BS 7671 details two voltage categories, Band 1 and Band 2. Band 1 is essentially Extra low voltage (ELV) systems and Band 2 Low voltage (LV) systems.

ELV is less than 50 V AC between conductors or to earth. LV exceeds ELV up to 1000 V AC between conductors and 600 V between conductors and earth.

The suppliers are now governed by the 'Electricity Safety, Quality & Continuity Regulations 2002' (formerly the Electricity Supply Regulations 1988).

CHAPTER 2

Earthing

☞ Relevant BS 7671 chapters and parts: Chapters 31, 41, 54, Part 7

DEFINITIONS USED IN THIS CHAPTER

Basic protection Protection against electric shock under fault-free conditions.

Bonding conductor A protective conductor providing equipotential bonding.

Circuit protective conductor (cpc) A protective conductor connecting exposed conductive parts of equipment to the main earthing terminal.

Earth The conductive mass of earth, whose electric potential at any point is conventionally taken as zero.

Earth electrode resistance The resistance of an earth electrode to earth.

Earth fault current An overcurrent resulting from a fault of negligible impedance between a line conductor and an exposed conductive part or a protective conductor.

Earth fault loop impedance The impedance of the phase-to-earth loop path starting and ending at the point of fault.

Earthing conductor A protective conductor connecting a main earthing terminal of an installation to an earth electrode or other means of earthing.

Equipotential bonding Electrical connection maintaining various exposed conductive parts and extraneous conductive parts at a substantially equal potential.

Exposed conductive part A conductive part of equipment which can be touched and which is not a live part but which may become live under fault conditions.

Extraneous conductive part A conductive part liable to introduce a potential, generally earth potential, and not forming part of the electrical installation.

Fault protection Protection against electric shock under single-fault conditions.

Functional earth Earthing of a point or points in a system or an installation or in equipment for purposes other than safety, such as for proper functioning of electrical equipment.

Leakage current Electric current in an unwanted conductive part under normal operating conditions.

Line conductor A conductor of an AC system for the transmission of electrical energy, other than a neutral conductor.

Live part A conductor or conductive part intended to be energized in normal use, including a neutral conductor but, by convention, not a PEN conductor.

PEN conductor A conductor combining the functions of both protective conductor and neutral conductor.

PME (protective multiple earthing) An earthing arrangement, found in TN-C-S systems, where an installation is earthed via the supply neutral conductor.

Protective conductor A conductor used for some measure of protection against electric shock and intended for connecting together any of the following parts:

exposed conductive parts
extraneous conductive parts
main earthing terminal
earth electrode(s)
earthed point of the source.

Residual current device (RCD) An electromechanical switching device or association of devices intended to cause the opening of the contacts when the residual current attains a given value under given conditions.

Simultaneously accessible parts Conductors or conductive parts which can be touched simultaneously by a person or, where applicable, by livestock.

EARTH: WHAT IT IS, AND WHY AND HOW WE CONNECT TO IT

The thin layer of material which covers our planet, be it rock, clay, chalk or whatever, is what we in the world of electricity refer to as earth. So, why do we need to connect anything to it? After all, it is not as if earth is a good conductor.

Perhaps it would be wise at this stage to investigate potential difference (PD). A PD is exactly what it says it is: a difference in potential (volts). Hence, two conductors having PDs of, say, 20 V and 26 V have a PD between them of $26 - 20 = 6$ V. The original PDs, i.e. 20 V and 26 V, are the PDs between 20 V and 0 V and 26 V and 0 V.

So where does this 0 V or zero potential come from? The simple answer is, in our case, the earth. The definition of earth is therefore the conductive mass of earth, whose electric potential at any point is conventionally taken as zero.

Hence, if we connect a voltmeter between a live part (e.g. the line conductor of, say, a socket outlet circuit) and earth, we may read

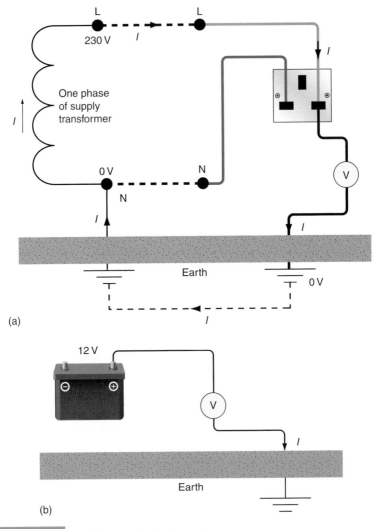

(a)

(b)

(a) Earth path, (b) No earth path.

230 V; the conductor is at 230 V, the earth at zero. The earth provides a path to complete the circuit. We would measure nothing at all if we connected our voltmeter between, say, the positive 12 V terminal of a car battery and earth, as in this case the earth plays no part in any circuit. Figure 2.1 illustrates this difference.

Hence, a person in an installation touching a live part whilst standing on the earth would take the place of the voltmeter in Figure 2.1a, and could suffer a severe electric shock. Remember that the accepted lethal level of shock current passing through a person is only 50 mA or 1/20 A. The same situation would arise if the person were touching, say, a faulty appliance and a gas or water pipe (Figure 2.2).

One method of providing some measure of protection against these effects is to join together (bond) all metallic parts and connect them to earth. This ensures that all metalwork in a healthy

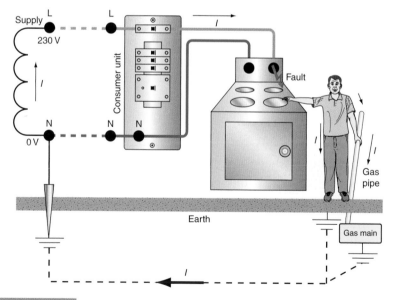

FIGURE 2.2 Shock path.

situation is at or near zero volts, and under fault conditions all metalwork will rise to a similar potential. So, simultaneous contact with two such metal parts would not result in a dangerous shock, as there will be no significant PD between them. This method is known as protective equipotential bonding.

Unfortunately, as previously mentioned, earth itself is not a good conductor unless it is very wet, and therefore it presents a high resistance to the flow of fault current. This resistance is usually enough to restrict fault current to a level well below that of the rating of the protective device, leaving a faulty circuit uninterrupted. Clearly this is an unhealthy situation. The methods of overcoming this problem will be dealt with later.

In all but the most rural areas, consumers can connect to a metallic earth return conductor which is ultimately connected to the earthed neutral of the supply. This, of course, presents a low-resistance path for fault currents to operate the protection.

Summarizing, then, connecting metalwork to earth places that metal at or near zero potential, and bonding between metallic parts puts such parts at a similar potential even under fault conditions.

Connecting to earth

In the light of previous comments, it is obviously necessary to have as low an earth path resistance as possible, and the point of connection to earth is one place where such resistance may be reduced. When two conducting surfaces are placed in contact with each other, there will be a resistance to the flow of current dependent on the surface areas in contact. It is clear, then, that the greater surface contact area with earth that can be achieved, the better.

There are several methods of making a connection to earth, including the use of rods, plates and tapes. By far the most popular method in everyday use is the rod earth electrode. The plate type needs to be buried at a sufficient depth to be effective and, as such plates may be 1 or 2 metres square, considerable excavation may be necessary. The tape type is predominantly used in the earthing of large electricity substations, where the tape is laid in trenches in a mesh formation over the whole site. Items of plant are then earthed to this mesh.

Rod electrodes

These are usually of solid copper or copper-clad carbon steel, the latter being used for the larger-diameter rods with extension facilities. These facilities comprise: a thread at each end of the rod to enable a coupler to be used for connection of the next rod; a steel cap to protect the thread from damage when the rod is being driven in; a steel driving tip; and a clamp for the connection of an earth tape or conductor (Figure 2.3).

The choice of length and diameter of such a rod will, as previously mentioned, depend on the soil conditions. For example, a long thick electrode is used for earth with little moisture retention. Generally, a 1–2 m rod, 16 mm in diameter, will give a relatively low resistance.

EARTH ELECTRODE RESISTANCE

If we were to place an electrode in the earth and then measure the resistance between the electrode and points at increasingly larger distance from it, we would notice that the resistance increased with distance until a point was reached (usually around 2.5 m) beyond which no increase in resistance was noticed (Figure 2.4, see page 25).

The resistance area around the electrode is particularly important with regard to the voltage at the surface of the ground (Figure 2.5, see page 26). For a 2 m rod, with its top at ground level, 80–90%

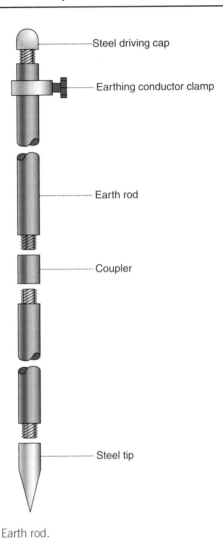

FIGURE 2.3   Earth rod.

of the voltage appearing at the electrode under fault conditions is dropped across the earth in the first 2.5 to 3 m. This is particularly dangerous where livestock is present, as the hind and fore legs of an animal can be respectively inside and outside the resistance area: a PD of 25 V can be lethal! One method of overcoming

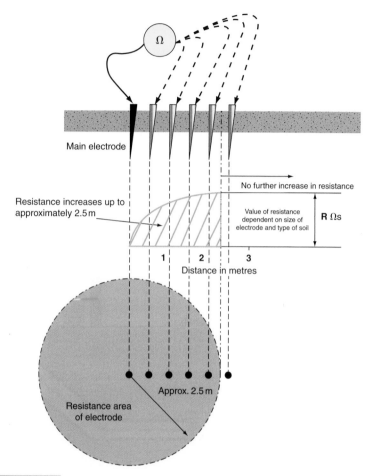

FIGURE 2.4   Earth electrode resistance area.

this problem is to house the electrode in a pit below ground level (Figure 2.6) as this prevents voltages appearing at ground level.

EARTHING IN THE IEE REGULATIONS (IEE REGULATIONS CHAPTER 4, SECTION 411)

In the preceding pages we have briefly discussed the reasons for, and the importance and methods of, earthing. Let us now examine the subject in relation to the IEE Regulations.

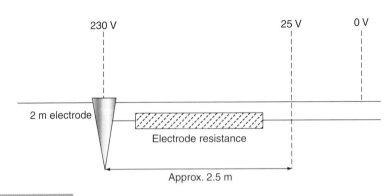

FIGURE 2.5

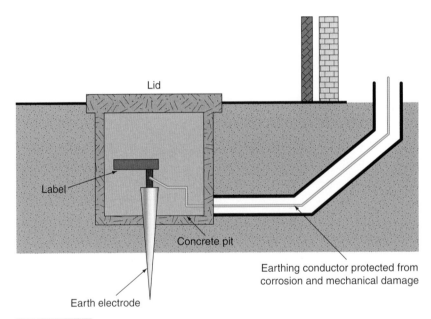

FIGURE 2.6 Earth electrode installation.

Contact with metalwork made live by a fault is clearly undesirable. One popular method of providing some measure of protection against the effects of such contact is by protective earthing, protective equipotential bonding and automatic disconnection in the event of a fault. This entails the bonding together and connection to earth of:

1. All metalwork associated with electrical apparatus and systems, termed exposed conductive parts. Examples include conduit, trunking and the metal cases of apparatus.
2. All metalwork liable to introduce a potential including earth potential, termed extraneous conductive parts. Examples are gas, oil and water pipes, structural steelwork, radiators, sinks and baths.

The conductors used in such connections are called *protective conductors*, and they can be further subdivided into:

1. Circuit protective conductors, for connecting exposed conductive parts to the main earthing terminal.
2. Main protective bonding conductors, for bonding together main incoming services, structural steelwork, etc.
3. Supplementary bonding conductors for bonding exposed conductive parts and extraneous conductive parts, when circuit disconnection times cannot be met, or in special locations, such as bathrooms, swimming pools, etc.

The effect of all this bonding is to create a zone in which all metalwork of different services and systems will, even under fault conditions, be at a substantially equal potential. If, added to this, there is a low-resistance earth return path, the protection should operate fast enough to prevent danger (IEE Regulations 411.3 to 411.6).

The resistance of such an earth return path will depend upon the system (see the next section), either TT, TN-S or TN-C-S (IT systems will not be discussed here, as they are extremely rare and unlikely to be encountered by the average contractor).

EARTHING SYSTEMS (IEE REGULATIONS DEFINITIONS (SYSTEMS))

These have been designated in the IEE Regulations using the letters T, N, C and S. These letters stand for:

T   terre (French for earth) and meaning a direct connection to earth

N   neutral

C   combined

S   separate.

When these letters are grouped they form the classification of a type of system. The first letter in such a classification denotes how the supply source is earthed. The second denotes how the metalwork of an installation is earthed. The third and fourth indicate the functions of neutral and protective conductors. Hence:

1. A TT system has a direct connection of the supply source neutral to earth and a direct connection of the installation metalwork to earth. An example is an overhead line supply with earth electrodes, and the mass of earth as a return path (Figure 2.7).

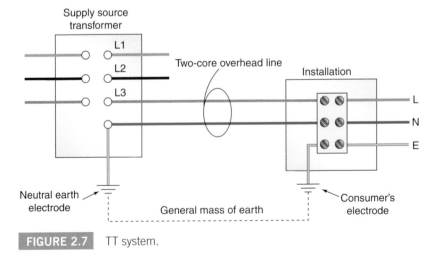

FIGURE 2.7   TT system.

2. A TN-S system has the supply source neutral directly
   connected to earth, the installation metalwork connected
   to the earthed neutral of the supply source via the lead
   sheath of the supply cable, and the neutral and protective
   conductors throughout the whole system performing
   separate functions (Figure 2.8).

3. A TN-C-S system is as the TN-S but the supply cable
   sheath is also the neutral, i.e. it forms a combined earth/
   neutral conductor known as a PEN (protective earthed
   neutral) conductor (Figure 2.9).

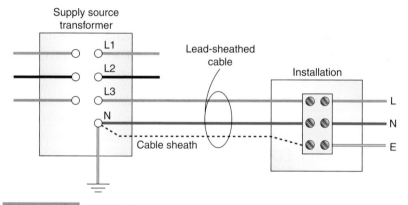

FIGURE 2.8   TN-S system.

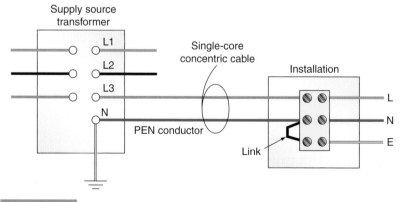

FIGURE 2.9   TN-C-S system.

The installation earth and neutral are separate conductors. This system is also known as PME.

Note that only single-phase systems have been shown, for simplicity.

Summary

In order to reduce the risk of serious electric shock, it is important to provide a path for earth fault currents to operate the circuit protection, and to endeavour to maintain all metalwork at a substantially equal potential. This is achieved by bonding together metalwork of electrical and non-electrical systems to earth. The path for earth fault currents would then be via the earth itself in TT systems or by a metallic return path in TN-S or TN-C-S systems.

EARTH FAULT LOOP IMPEDANCE

As we have seen, circuit protection should operate in the event of a direct fault from line to earth (automatic disconnection). The speed of operation of the protection is extremely important and will depend on the magnitude of the fault current, which in turn will depend on the impedance of the earth fault loop path, Z_s.

Figure 2.10 shows this path. Starting at the fault, the path comprises:

1. The cpc.
2. The consumer's earthing terminal and earth conductor.
3. The return path, either metallic or earth, dependent on the earthing system.
4. The earthed neutral of the supply transformer.

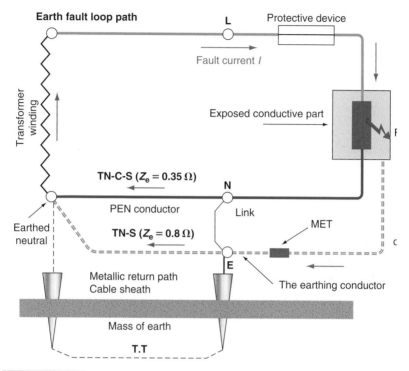

FIGURE 2.10 Earth fault loop path.

5. The transformer winding.
6. The line conductor from the transformer to the fault.

Figure 2.11 is a simplified version of this path. We have:

$$Z_s = Z_e + R_1 + R_2$$

where Z_s is the actual total loop impedance, Z_e is the loop impedance external to the installation, R_1 is the resistance of the line
conductor, and R_2 is the resistance of the cpc. We also have:

$$I = U_0/Z_s$$

where I is the fault current and U_0 is the nominal line voltage to
earth.

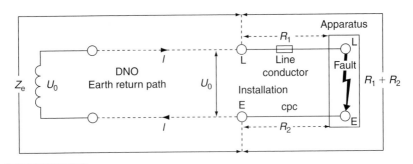

FIGURE 2.11   Simplified loop path.

DETERMINING THE VALUE OF TOTAL LOOP IMPEDANCE

The IEE Regulations require that when the general characteristics of an installation are assessed, the loop impedance Z_e external to the installation shall be ascertained.

This may be measured in existing installations using a line-to-earth loop impedance tester. However, when a building is only at the drawing board stage it is clearly impossible to make such a measurement. In this case, we have three methods available to assess the value of Z_s:

1. Determine it from details (if available) of the supply transformer, the main distribution cable and the proposed service cable; or
2. Measure it from the supply intake position of an adjacent building having service cable of similar size and length to that proposed; or
3. Use maximum likely values issued by the supply authority as follows:

   TT system: $21\,\Omega$ maximum

   TN-S system: $0.80\,\Omega$ maximum

   TN-C-S system: $0.35\,\Omega$ maximum.

Method 1 will be difficult for anyone except engineers. Method 3 can, in some cases, result in pessimistically large cable sizes. Method 2, if it is possible to be used, will give a closer and more realistic estimation of Z_e. However, if in any doubt, use method 3.

Having established a value for Z_e, it is now necessary to determine the impedance of that part of the loop path internal to the installation. This is, as we have seen, the resistance of the line conductor plus the resistance of the cpc, i.e. $R_1 + R_2$. Resistances of copper conductors may be found from manufacturers' information which gives values of resistance/metre for copper and aluminium conductors at 20°C in mΩ/m. Table 2.1 gives resistance values for copper conductors up to 35 mm^2.

Table 2.1 Resistance of Copper Conductors at 20°C.

Conductor CSA (mm²)	Resistance (mΩ/m)
1.0	18.1
1.5	12.1
2.5	7.41
4.0	4.61
6.0	3.08
10.0	1.83
16.0	1.15
25.0	0.727
35.0	0.524

A 25 mm^2 line conductor with a 4 mm^2 cpc has $R_1 = 0.727$ and $R_2 = 4.61$, giving $R_1 + R_2 = 0.727 + 4.61 = 5.337$ mΩ/m. So, having established a value for $R_1 + R_2$, we must now multiply it by the length of the run and divide by 1000 (the values given are in mΩ/m). However, this final value is based on a temperature of 20°C, but when the conductor is fully loaded its temperature will increase. In order to determine the value of resistance at conductor operating temperature, a multiplier is used.

This multiplier, applied to the 20°C value of resistance, is determined from the following formula:

$$R_t = R_{20}\{1 + \alpha_{20}(\theta - 20)\}$$

where

R_t = the resistance at conductor operating temperature
R_{20} = the resistance at 20°C
α_{20} = the 20°C temperature coefficient of copper,
      0.004 Ω/Ω/°C
θ = the conductor operating temperature.

Clearly, the multiplier is $\{1 + \alpha_{20}(\theta - 20)\}$.

So, for a 70°C thermoplastic insulated conductor (Table 54C IEE Regulations), the multiplier becomes:

$$\{1 + 0.004(70° - 20°)\} = 1.2$$

And for a 90°C XLPE type cable it becomes:

$$\{1 + 0.004(90° - 20°)\} = 1.28$$

Hence, for a 20 m length of 70°C PVC insulated 16 mm² line conductor with a 4 mm² cpc, the value of $R_1 + R_2$ would be:

$$R_1 + R_2 = [(1.15 + 4.61) \times 20 \times 1.2]/1000 = 0.138\ \Omega$$

We are now in a position to determine the total earth fault loop impedance Z_s from:

$$Z_s = Z_e + R_1 + R_2$$

As previously mentioned, this value of Z_s should be as low as possible to allow enough fault current to flow to operate the protection as quickly as possible. Tables 41.2, 41.3 and 41.4 of the IEE Regulations give maximum values of loop impedance for different sizes and types of protection for both final circuits, and distribution circuits.

Provided that the actual values calculated do not exceed those tabulated, final circuits up to 32 A will disconnect under earth fault conditions in 0.4 s or less, and distribution circuits in 5 s or less. The reasoning behind these different times is based on the time that a faulty circuit can reasonably be left uninterrupted. Hence, socket outlet circuits from which hand-held appliances may be used clearly present a greater shock risk than distribution circuits. It should be noted that these times, i.e. 0.4 s and 5 s, do not indicate the duration that a person can be in contact with a fault. They are based on the probable chances of someone being in contact with exposed or extraneous conductive parts at the precise moment that a fault develops.

☞ See also Table 41.1 of the IEE Regulations.

Example 2.1

Let us now have a look at a typical example of, say, a shower circuit run in an 18 m length of 6.0 mm² (6242 Y) twin cable with cpc, and protected by a 30 A BS 3036 semi-enclosed rewirable fuse. A 6.0 mm² twin cable has a 2.5 mm² cpc. We will also assume that the external loop impedance Z_e is measured as 0.27 Ω. Will there be a shock risk if a line-to-earth fault occurs?

The total loop impedance $Z_s = Z_e + R_1 + R_2$. We are given $Z_e = 0.27 \, \Omega$.

For a 6.0 mm² line conductor with a 2.5 mm² cpc, $R_1 + R_2$ is 10.49 mΩ/m. Hence, with a multiplier of 1.2 for 70°C PVC,

$$\text{total } R_1 + R_2 = 18 \times 10.49 \times 1.2 / 1000 = 0.23 \, \Omega$$

Therefore, $Z_s = 0.27 + 0.23 = 0.5 \, \Omega$. This is less than the 1.09 Ω maximum given in Table 41.2 for a 30 A BS 3036 fuse. Hence, the protection will disconnect the circuit in less than 0.4 s. In fact it will disconnect in less than 0.1 s; the determination of this time will be dealt with in Chapter 5.

Example 2.2

Consider, now, a more complex installation, and note how the procedure remains unchanged.

In this example, a three-phase motor is fed using 25 mm² single PVC conductors in trunking, the cpc being 2.5 mm². The circuit is protected by BS 1361 45 A fuses in a distribution fuseboard. The distribution circuit or sub-main feeding this fuseboard comprises 70 mm² PVC singles in trunking with a 25 mm² cpc, the protection being by BS 88 160 A fuses. The external loop impedance Z_e has a measured value of 0.2 Ω. Will this circuit arrangement comply with the shock-risk constraints?

The formula $Z_s = Z_e + R_1 + R_2$ must be extended, as the $(R_1 + R_2)$ component comprises both the distribution and motor circuits; it therefore becomes:

$$Z_s = Z_e + (R_1 + R_2)_1 + (R_1 + R_2)_2$$

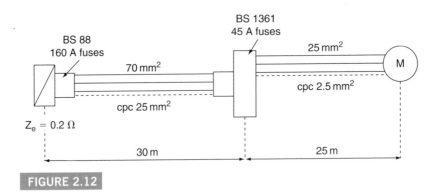

FIGURE 2.12

Distribution circuit $(R_1 + R_2)_1$

This comprises 30 m of 70 mm² line conductor and 30 m of 25 mm² cpc. Typical values for conductors over 35 mm² are shown in Table 2.2.

As an alternative we can use our knowledge of the relationship between conductor resistance and area, e.g. a 10 mm² conductor

Table 2.2

Area of Conductor (mm²)	Resistance (mΩ/m) Copper	Aluminium
50	0.387	0.641
70	0.263	0.443
95	0.193	0.320
120	0.153	0.253
185	0.0991	0.164
240	0.0754	0.125
300	0.0601	0.1

has approximately 10 times less resistance than a $1.0\,\text{mm}^2$ conductor:

$$10\,\text{mm}^2 \text{ resistance } = 1.83\,\text{m}\Omega/\text{m}$$
$$1.0\,\text{mm}^2 \text{ resistance } = 18.1\,\text{m}\Omega/\text{m}$$

Hence a $70\,\text{mm}^2$ conductor will have a resistance approximately half that of a $35\,\text{mm}^2$ conductor:

$$35\,\text{mm}^2 \text{ resistance } = 0.524\,\text{m}\Omega/\text{m}$$

$$\therefore 70\,\text{mm}^2 \text{ resistance } = \frac{0.524}{2} = 0.262\,\text{m}\Omega/\text{m}$$

which compares well with the value given in Table 2.2.

$$25\,\text{mm}^2 \text{ cpc resistance } = 0.727\,\text{m}\Omega/\text{m}$$

so the distribution circuit

$$(R_1 + R_2)_1 = 30 \times (0.262 + 0.727) \times 1.2 / 1000 = 0.035\,\Omega$$

Hence $Z_s = Z_e + (R_1 + R_2)_1 = 0.2 + 0.035 = 0.235\,\Omega$, which is less than the Z_s maximum of $0.25\,\Omega$ quoted for a $160\,\text{A}$ BS 88 fuse in Table 41.3 of the Regulations.

Motor circuit $(R_1 + R_2)_2$

Here we have 25 m of 25 mm^2 line conductor with 25 m of 2.5 mm^2 cpc. Hence:

$$(R_1 + R_2)_2 = 25 \times (0.727 + 7.41) \times 1.2/1000$$
$$= 0.24\,\Omega$$

$$\therefore \text{Total } Z_s = Z_e + (R_1 + R_2)_1 + (R_1 + R_2)_2$$
$$= 0.2 + 0.035 + 0.24 = 0.48\,\Omega$$

which is less than the Z_s maximum of $0.96\,\Omega$ quoted for a 45 A BS 1361 fuse from Table 41.3 of the Regulations. Hence we have achieved compliance with the shock-risk constraints.

ADDITIONAL PROTECTION

Residual current devices

The following list indicates the ratings and uses of RCDs detailed in BS 7671.

Requirements for RCD protection

30 mA

- All socket outlets rated at not more than 20 A and for un-supervised general use
- Mobile equipment rated at not more than 32 A for use outdoors
- All circuits in a bath/shower room
- Preferred for all circuits in a TT system
- All cables installed less than 50 mm from the surface of a wall or partition (in the safe zones) if the installation is unsupervised, and also at any depth if the construction of the wall or partition includes metallic parts

- In zones 0, 1 and 2 of swimming pool locations
- All circuits in a location containing saunas, etc.
- Socket outlet final circuits not exceeding 32 A in agricultural locations
- Circuits supplying Class II equipment in restrictive conductive locations
- Each socket outlet in caravan parks and marinas and final circuit for houseboats
- All socket outlet circuits rated not more than 32 A for show stands, etc.
- All socket outlet circuits rated not more than 32 A for construction sites (where reduced low voltage, etc. is not used)
- All socket outlets supplying equipment outside mobile or transportable units
- All circuits in caravans
- All circuits in circuses, etc.
- A circuit supplying Class II heating equipment for floor and ceiling heating systems.

100 mA

- Socket outlets of rating exceeding 32 A in agricultural locations.

300 mA

- At the origin of a temporary supply to circuses, etc.
- Where there is a risk of fire due to storage of combustible materials
- All circuits (except socket outlets) in agricultural locations.

500 mA

- Any circuit supplying one or more socket outlets of rating exceeding 32 A, on a construction site.

We have seen the importance of the total earth loop impedance Z_s in the reduction of shock risk.

However, in some systems and especially TT, where the maximum values of Z_s given in Tables 41.2, 41.3 and 41.4 of the Regulations may be hard to satisfy, an RCD may be used: its residual rating being determined from:

$$I_{\Delta n} \leq 50/Z_s$$

Principle of operation of an RCD

Figure 2.13 illustrates the construction of an RCD. In a healthy circuit the same current passes through the line coil, the load, and back through the neutral coil. Hence the magnetic effects of line and neutral currents cancel out.

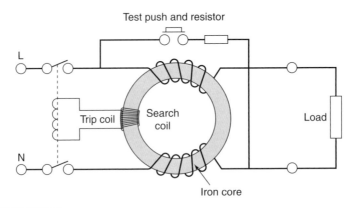

FIGURE 2.13 Residual current device.

In a faulty circuit, either line to earth or neutral to earth, these currents are no longer equal. Therefore the out-of-balance current produces some residual magnetism in the core. As this magnetism is alternating, it links with the turns of the search coil, inducing an electro-motive force (EMF) in it. This EMF in turn drives a current through the trip coil, causing operation of the tripping mechanism.

It should be noted that a line-to-neutral fault will appear as a load, and hence the RCD will not operate for this fault.

A three-phase RCD works on the same out-of-balance principle; in this case the currents flowing in the three lines when they are all equal sum to zero, hence there is no resultant magnetism. Even if they are unequal, the out-of-balance current flows in the neutral which cancels out this out-of-balance current. Figure 2.14 shows the arrangement of a three-phase RCD, and Figure 2.15 how it can be connected for use on single-phase circuits.

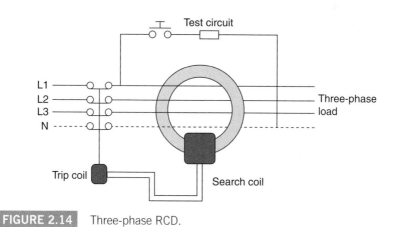

FIGURE 2.14   Three-phase RCD.

Nuisance tripping

Certain appliances such as cookers, water heaters and freezers tend to have, by the nature of their construction and use, some leakage currents to earth. These are quite normal, but could cause the operation of an RCD protecting an entire installation. This can be overcome by using split-load consumer units, where socket outlet

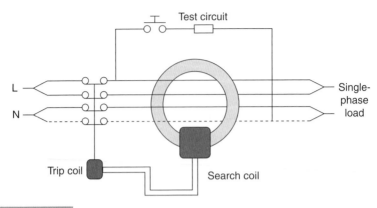

Test circuit

L

N

Single-phase load

Trip coil

Search coil

FIGURE 2.15 Connections for single phase.

circuits are protected by a 30 mA RCD, leaving all other circuits controlled by a normal mains switch. Better still, especially in TT systems, is the use of a 100 mA RCD for protecting circuits other than socket outlets.

Modern developments in CB, RCD and consumer unit design now make it easy to protect any individual circuit with a combined CB/RCD (RCBO), making the use of split-load boards unnecessary.

An exception to the 30 mA RCD requirement for socket outlet circuits can be achieved by providing an indication that a particular socket outlet or outlets are not for general use, e.g. freezers, etc. This, of course, means the installation of a separate non-RCD protected circuit.

Supplementary bonding (IEE Regulations Section 415.2)

In general the only Supplementary bonding required is for special locations such as bathrooms (not always needed – see Chapter 7), swimming pools, agricultural premises, etc. and where disconnection times cannot be met.

By now we should know why bonding is necessary; the next question, however, is to what extent bonding should be carried out. This is perhaps answered best by means of question and answer examples:

1. **Do I need to bond the hot and cold taps and a metal kitchen sink together? Surely they are all joined anyway?**

   Provided that main protective bonding conductors have been correctly installed there is no specific requirement in BS 7671 to do this.

2. **Do I have to bond radiators in a premises to, say, metal-clad switches or socket outlets, etc.?**

   Supplementary bonding is only necessary when extraneous conductive parts are simultaneously accessible with exposed conductive parts and the disconnection time for the circuit concerned cannot be achieved. In these circumstances the bonding conductor should have a resistance $R \leqslant 50/I_a$, where I_a is the operating current of the protection.

3. **Do I need to bond metal window frames?**

   In general, no. Apart from the fact that most window frames will not introduce a potential from anywhere, the part of the window most likely to be touched is the opening portion, to which it would not be practicable to bond. There may be a case for the bonding if the frames were fortuitously touching structural steel work.

4. **What about bonding in bathrooms?**

   Refer to Chapter 7.

5. **What size of bonding conductors should I use?**

   Main protective bonding conductors should be not less than half the size of the main earthing conductor, subject to a minimum of 60 mm² or, where PME (TN-C-S) conditions are

present, $10.0\,mm^2$. For example, most new domestic installations now have a $16.0\,mm^2$ earthing conductor, so all main
bonding will be in $10.0\,mm^2$. Supplementary bonding conductors are subject to a minimum of $2.5\,mm^2$ if mechanically
protected or $4.0\,mm^2$ if not. However, if these bonding conductors are connected to exposed conductive parts, they must be
the same size as the cpc connected to the exposed conductive
part, once again subject to the minimum sizes mentioned. It is
sometimes difficult to protect a bonding2 conductor mechanically throughout its length, and especially at terminations, so it
is perhaps better to use $4.0\,mm^2$ as the minimum size.

6. **Do I have to bond free-standing metal cabinets, screens,
   workbenches, etc.?**
   No. These items will not introduce a potential into the equipotential zone from outside, and cannot therefore be regarded as
   extraneous conductive parts.

The Faraday cage

In one of his many experiments, Michael Faraday (1791–1867)
placed an assistant in an open-sided cube which was then covered in a conducting material and insulated from the floor. When
this cage arrangement was charged to a high voltage, the assistant found that he could move freely within it, touching any of the
sides, with no adverse effects. Faraday had, in fact, created an equipotential zone, and of course in a correctly bonded installation, we
live and/or work in Faraday cages!

CHAPTER 3

Protection

☞ Relevant IEE parts, chapters and sections: Part 4, Chapters 41, 42, 43, 44; Part 5, Chapter 53

DEFINITIONS USED IN THIS CHAPTER

Arm's reach A zone of accessibility to touch, extending from any point on a surface where persons usually stand or move about, to the limits which a person can reach with his hand in any direction without assistance.

Barrier A part providing a defined degree of protection against contact with live parts, from any usual direction.

Basic protection Protection against electric shock under fault-free conditions.

Circuit protective conductor A protective conductor connecting exposed conductive parts of equipment to the main earthing terminal.

Class II equipment Equipment in which protection against electric shock does not rely on basic insulation only, but in which additional safety precautions such as supplementary insulation are provided. There is no provision for the connection of exposed metalwork of the equipment to a protective conductor, and no reliance upon precautions to be taken in the fixed wiring of the installation.

Design current The magnitude of the current intended to be carried by a circuit in normal service.

Enclosure A part providing an appropriate degree of protection of equipment against certain external influences and a defined degree of protection against contact with live parts from any direction.

Exposed conductive part A conductive part of equipment which can be touched and which is not a live part but which may become live under fault conditions.

External influence Any influence external to an electrical installation which affects the design and safe operation of that installation.

Extraneous conductive part A conductive part liable to introduce a potential, generally earth potential, and not forming part of the electrical installation.

Fault current A current resulting from a fault.

Fault Protection Protection against electric shock under single fault conditions.

Insulation Suitable non-conductive mate rial enclosing, surrounding or supporting a conductor.

Isolation Cutting off an electrical installation, a circuit or an item of equipment from every source of electrical energy.

Live part A conductor or conductive part intended to be energized in normal use, including a neutral conductor but, by convention, not a PEN conductor.

Obstacle A part preventing unintentional contact with live parts but not preventing deliberate contact.

Overcurrent A current exceeding the rated value. For conductors the rated value is the current-carrying capacity.

Overload An overcurrent occurring in a circuit which is electrically sound.

Residual current device (RCD) An electromechanical switching device or association of devices intended to cause the opening of the contacts when the residual current attains a given value under specified conditions.

Short-circuit current An overcurrent resulting from a fault of negligible impedance between live conductors having a difference of potential under normal operating conditions.

Skilled person A person with technical knowledge or sufficient experience to enable him to avoid the dangers which electricity may create.

WHAT IS PROTECTION?

The meaning of the word 'protection', as used in the electrical industry, is no different to that in everyday use. People protect themselves against personal or financial loss by means of insurance and from injury or discomfort by the use of the correct protective clothing. They further protect their property by the installation of security measures such as locks and/or alarm systems. In the same way, electrical systems need:

1. to be protected against mechanical damage, the effects of the environment and electrical overcurrents; and
2. to be installed in such a fashion that persons and/or livestock are protected from the dangers that such an electrical installation may create.

Let us now look at these protective measures in more detail.

Protection against mechanical damage

The word 'mechanical' is somewhat misleading in that most of us associate it with machinery of some sort. In fact, a serious electrical overcurrent left uninterrupted for too long can cause distortion of conductors and degradation of insulation; both of these effects are considered to be mechanical damage.

However, let us start by considering the ways of preventing mechanical damage by physical impact and the like.

Cable construction

A cable comprises one or more conductors each covered with an insulating material. This insulation provides protection from shock by contact with live parts and prevents the passage of leakage currents between conductors.

Clearly, insulation is very important and in itself should be protected from damage. This may be achieved by covering the insulated conductors with a protective sheathing during manufacture, or by enclosing them in conduit or trunking at the installation stage.

The type of sheathing chosen and/or the installation method will depend on the environment in which the cable is to be installed. For example, metal conduit with thermoplastic (PVC) singles or mineral-insulated (MI) cable would be used in preference to PVC-sheathed cable clipped direct, in an industrial environment. Figure 3.1 shows the effect of physical impact on MI cable.

Protection against corrosion

Mechanical damage to cable sheaths and metalwork of wiring systems can occur through corrosion, and hence care must be

FIGURE 3.1   MI cable. On impact, all parts including the conductors are flattened, and a proportionate thickness of insulation remains between conductors, and conductors and sheath, without impairing the performance of the cable at normal working voltages.

taken to choose corrosion-resistant materials and to avoid contact between dissimilar metals in damp situations.

Protection against thermal effects

This is the subject of Chapter 42 of the IEE Regulations. Basically, it requires common-sense decisions regarding the placing of fixed equipment, such that surrounding materials are not at risk from damage by heat.

Added to these requirements is the need to protect persons from burns by guarding parts of equipment liable to exceed temperatures listed in Table 42.1 of the Regulations.

Polyvinyl chloride

PVC is a thermoplastic polymer widely used in electrical installation work for cable insulation, conduit and trunking. General-purpose PVC is manufactured to the British Standard BS 6746.

PVC in its raw state is a white powder; it is only after the addition of plasticizers and stabilizers that it acquires the form that we are familiar with.

Degradation

All PVC polymers are degraded or reduced in quality by heat and light. Special stabilizers added during manufacture help to retard this degradation at high temperatures. However, it is recommended that PVC-sheathed cables or thermoplastic fittings for luminaires (light fittings) should not be installed where the temperature is likely to rise above 60°C. Cables insulated with high-temperature PVC (up to 80°C) should be used for drops to lampholders and entries into batten-holders. PVC conduit and trunking should not be used in temperatures above 60°C.

Embrittlement and cracking

PVC exposed to low temperatures becomes brittle and will easily crack if stressed. Although both rigid and flexible, PVC used in cables and conduit can reach as low as 5°C without becoming brittle; it is recommended that general-purpose PVC-insulated cables should not be installed in areas where the temperature is likely to be consistently below 0°C, and that PVC-insulated cable should not be handled unless the ambient temperature is above 0°C and unless the cable temperature has been above 0°C for at least 24 hours.

Where rigid PVC conduit is to be installed in areas where the ambient temperature is below −5°C but not lower than −25°C, type B conduit manufactured to BS 4607 should be used.

When PVC-insulated cables are installed in loft spaces insulated with polystyrene granules, contact between the two polymers can cause the plasticizer in the PVC to migrate to the granules. This causes the PVC to harden and, although there is no change in the electrical properties, the insulation may crack if disturbed.

External influences

Appendix 5 of the IEE Regulations classifies external influences which may affect an installation. This classification is divided into three sections, the environment (A), how that environment is utilized (B) and construction of buildings (C). The nature of any influence within each section is also represented by a letter, and the level of influence by a number. Table 3.1 gives examples of the classification.

Table 3.1   Examples of Classifications of External Influences.

Environment	Utilization	Building
Water	Capability	Materials
AD6 Waves	**BA3** Handicapped	**CA1** Non-combustible

With external influences included on drawings and in specifications, installations and materials used can be designed accordingly.

Protection against ingress of solid objects, liquid and impact

In order to protect equipment from damage by foreign bodies, liquid or impact and also to prevent persons from coming into contact with live or moving parts, such equipment is housed inside enclosures or cable management systems such as conduit, trunking ducts, etc.

The degree of protection offered by such an enclosure is the subject of BS EN 60529 and BS EN 62262, commonly known as the IP and IK codes, parts of which are as shown in the accompanying tables. It will be seen from the IP table that, for instance, an enclosure to IP56 is dustproof and waterproof (Tables 3.2 and 3.3).

The most commonly quoted IP codes in the Regulations are IPXXB and IP2X (the X denotes that no protection is specified, *not* that no protection exists).

Table 3.2 IP Codes.

First numeral: Mechanical protection

0. No protection of persons against contact with live or moving parts inside the enclosure. No protection of equipment against ingress of solid foreign bodies.

1. Protection against accidental or inadvertent contact with live or moving parts inside the enclosure by a large surface of the human body, for example a hand, not for protection against deliberate access to such parts. Protection against ingress of large solid foreign bodies.

2. Protection against contact with live or moving parts inside the enclosure by fingers. Protection against ingress of medium-sized solid foreign bodies.

3. Protection against contact with live or moving parts inside the enclosure by tools, wires or such objects of thickness greater than 2.5 mm. Protection against ingress of small foreign bodies.

4. Protection against contact with live or moving parts inside the enclosure by tools, wires or such objects of thickness greater than 1 mm. Protection against ingress of small foreign bodies.

5. Complete protection against contact with live or moving parts inside the enclosures. Protection against harmful deposits of dust. The ingress of dust is not totally prevented, but dust cannot enter in an amount sufficient to interfere with satisfactory operation of the equipment enclosed.

6. Complete protection against contact with live or moving parts inside the enclosures. Protection against ingress of dust.

Second numeral: Liquid protection

0. No protection.

1. Protection against drops of condensed water. Drops of condensed water falling on the enclosure shall have no effect.

2. Protection against drops of liquid. Drops of falling liquid shall have no harmful effect when the enclosure is tilted at any angle up to 15° from the vertical.

3. Protection against rain. Water falling in rain at an angle equal to or smaller than 60° with respect to the vertical shall have no harmful effect.

4. Protection against splashing. Liquid splashed from any direction shall have no harmful effect.

5. Protection against water jets. Water projected by a nozzle from any direction under stated conditions shall have no harmful effect.

6. Protection against conditions on ships' decks (deck with watertight equipment). Water from heavy seas shall not enter the enclosures under prescribed conditions.

7. Protection against immersion in water. It must not be possible for water to enter the enclosure under stated conditions of pressure and time.

8. Protection against indefinite immersion in water under specified pressure. It must not be possible for water to enter the enclosure.

X Indicates no *specified* protections.

Table 3.3   IK Codes – Protection Against Mechanical Impact.

Code		
00		No protection
01 to 05		Impact < 1 joule
06	500 g 20 cm	Impact 1 joule
07	500 g 40 cm	Impact 2 joules
08	1.7 kg 29.5 cm	Impact 5 joules
09	5 kg 20 cm	Impact 10 joules
10	5 kg 40 cm	Impact 20 joules

Hence, IP2X means that an enclosure can withstand the ingress of medium-sized solid foreign bodies (12.5 mm diameter), and a jointed test finger, known affectionately as the British Standard finger! IPXXB denotes protection against the test finger only.

For accessible horizontal top surfaces of enclosures the IP codes are IPXXD and IP4X. This indicates protection against small foreign bodies and a 1 mm diameter test wire. IPXXD is the 1 mm diameter wire only.

IEE Regulations Section 522 give details of the types of equipment, cables, enclosure, etc. that may be selected for certain environmental conditions, e.g. an enclosure housing equipment in an AD8 environment (under water) would need to be to IPX8.

PROTECTION AGAINST ELECTRIC SHOCK (IEE REGULATIONS CHAPTER 41)

There are two ways of receiving an electric shock: by contact with intentionally live parts, and by contact with conductive parts made live due to a fault. It is obvious that we need to provide protection against both of these conditions.

Basic protection (IEE Regulations Sections 410 to 417)

Clearly, it is not satisfactory to have live parts accessible to touch by persons or livestock. The IEE Regulations recommend five ways of minimizing this danger:

1. By covering the live part or parts with insulation which can only be removed by destruction, e.g. cable insulation.

2. By placing the live part or parts behind a barrier or inside an enclosure providing protection to at least IPXXB or IP2X. In most cases, during the life of an installation it becomes necessary to open an enclosure or remove a barrier. Under these circumstances, this action should only be possible by the use of a key or tool, e.g. by using a screwdriver to open a junction box. Alternatively, access should only be gained

after the supply to the live parts has been disconnected, e.g. by isolation on the front of a control panel where the cover cannot be removed until the isolator is in the 'off' position. An intermediate barrier of at least IP2X or IPXXB will give protection when an enclosure is opened: a good example of this is the barrier inside distribution fuseboards, preventing accidental contact with incoming live feeds.

3. By placing obstacles to prevent unintentional approach to or contact with live parts. This method must only be used where skilled persons are working.

4. By placing out of arm's reach: for example, the high level of the bare conductors of travelling cranes.

5. By using an RCD as additional protection. Whilst not permitted as the sole means of protection, this is considered to reduce the risk associated with contact with live parts, provided that one of the other methods just mentioned is applied, and that the RCD has a rated operating current $I_{\Delta n}$ of not more than 30 mA and an operating time not exceeding 40 ms at 5 times I_n, i.e. 150 mA.

Fault protection (IEE Regulations Sections 410 to 417)

Protective earthing, protective equipotential bonding and automatic disconnection in the event of a fault have already been discussed in Chapter 2. The other methods are as follows.

Protection by automatic disconnection of supply (IEE Regulations Section 411)

This measure is a combination of basic and fault protection.

Double or reinforced insulation

Often referred to as Class II equipment, this is typical of modern appliances where there is no provision for the connection of a cpc.

This does not mean that there should be no exposed conductive parts and that the casing of equipment should be of an insulating material; it simply indicates that live parts are so well insulated that faults from live to conductive parts cannot occur.

Non-conducting location (IEE Regulations Section 418)

This is basically an area in which the floor, walls and ceiling are all insulated. Within such an area there must be no protective conductors, and socket outlets will have no earthing connections.

It must not be possible simultaneously to touch two exposed conductive parts, or an exposed conductive part and an extraneous conductive part. This requirement clearly prevents shock current passing through a person in the event of an earth fault, and the insulated construction prevents shock current passing to earth.

Earth-free local equipotential bonding (IEE Regulations Section 418)

This is, in essence, a Faraday cage, where all metal is bonded together but not to earth. Obviously great care must be taken when entering such a zone in order to avoid differences in potential between inside and outside.

The areas mentioned in this and the previous method are very uncommon. Where they do exist, they should be under constant supervision to ensure that no additions or alterations can lessen the protection intended.

Electrical separation (IEE Regulations Section 418)

This method relies on a supply from a safety source such as an isolating transformer to BS EN 60742 which has no earth connection

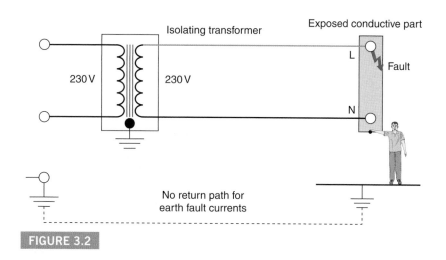

Isolating transformer

Exposed conductive part

230 V   230 V

L

Fault

N

No return path for
earth fault currents

FIGURE 3.2

on the secondary side. In the event of a circuit that is supplied from a source developing a live fault to an exposed conductive part, there would be no path for shock current to flow: see Figure 3.2.

Once again, great care must be taken to maintain the integrity of this type of system, as an inadvertent connection to earth, or interconnection with other circuits, would render the protection useless.

Exemptions (IEE Regulations 410.3.9)

As with most sets of rules and regulations, there are certain areas which are exempt from the requirements. These are listed quite clearly in IEE Regulations 410.3.9, and there is no point in repeating them all here. However, one example is the dispensing of the need to earth exposed conductive parts such as small fixings, screws and rivets, provided that they cannot be touched or gripped by a major part of the human body (not less than 50 mm by 50 mm), and that it is difficult to make and maintain an earth connection.

SELV or PELV

This is simply extra low voltage (less than 50 V AC) derived from a safety source such as a Class II safety isolating transformer to BS EN 61558-2-6; or a motor generator which has the same degree of isolation as the transformer; or a battery or diesel generator; or an electronic device such as a signal generator.

Live or exposed conductive parts of separated extra low voltage (SELV) circuits should not be connected to earth, or protective conductors of other circuits, and SELV or PELV circuit conductors should ideally be kept separate from those of other circuits. If this is not possible, then the SELV conductors should be insulated to the highest voltage present.

Obviously, plugs and sockets of SELV or PELV circuits should not be interchangeable with those of other circuits.

SELV or PELV circuits supplying socket outlets are mainly used for hand lamps or soldering irons, for example, in schools and colleges. Perhaps a more common example of an SELV or PELV circuit is a domestic bell installation, where the transformer is to BS EN 60742. Note that bell wire is usually only suitable for 50–60 V, which means that it should not be run together with circuit cables of higher voltages.

Reduced low-voltage systems (IEE Regulations Section 411.8)

The Health and Safety Executive accepts that a voltage of 65 V to earth, three-phase, or 55 V to earth, single-phase, will give protection against severe electric shock. They therefore recommend that portable tools used on construction sites, etc. be fed from a 110 V centre-tapped transformer. Figure 3.3 shows how 55 V is derived. Earth fault loop impedance values for these systems may be taken from Table 41.6 of the Regulations.

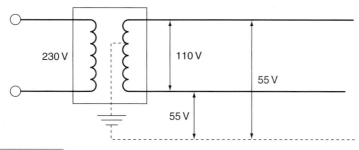

FIGURE 3.3

PROTECTION AGAINST OVERCURRENT (IEE REGULATIONS CHAPTER 43 AND DEFINITIONS)

An overcurrent is a current greater than the rated current of a circuit. It may occur in two ways:

1. As an overload current; or
2. As a fault current, which may be sub divided into:
   (a) A short-circuit current and
   (b) An earth fault current.

These conditions need to be protected against in order to avoid damage to circuit conductors and equipment. In practice, fuses and circuit breakers will fulfil both of these needs.

Overloads

Overloads are overcurrents occurring in healthy circuits. They may be caused, for example, by faulty appliances or by surges due to motors starting or by plugging in too many appliances in a socket outlet circuit.

Short circuits and earth faults

A short-circuit current is the current that will flow when a 'dead short' occurs between live conductors (line-to-neutral for single-phase; line-to-line for three-phase). Earth fault current flows when there is a short between a line conductor and earth. Prospective short-circuit current (PSCC) and prospective earth fault current (PEFC) are collectively known as prospective fault current (PFC). The term is usually used to signify the value of fault current at fuse or circuit breaker positions.

PFC is of great importance. However, before discussing it or any other overcurrent further, it is perhaps wise to refresh our memories with regard to fuses and circuit breakers and their characteristics.

Fuses and circuit breakers

As we all know, a fuse is the weak link in a circuit which will break when too much current flows, thus protecting the circuit conductors from damage.

There are many different types and sizes of fuse, all designed to perform a certain function. The IEE Regulations refer to only four of these: BS 3036, BS 88, BS 1361 and BS 1362 fuses. It is perhaps sensible to include, at this point, circuit breakers to BS 3871 and BS EN 60898.

Breaking capacity of fuses and circuit breakers (IEE Regulations Section 434)

When a fault occurs, the current may, for a fraction of a second, reach hundreds or even thousands of amperes. The protective device must be able to break and, in the case of circuit breakers, make such a current without damage to its surroundings by arcing, overheating or the scattering of hot particles.

Tables 3.4 and 3.5 indicate the performance of circuit breakers and the more commonly used British Standard fuse links.

Although all reference to BS 3871 MCBs have been removed from BS 7671, they are still used and therefore worthy of mention.

Table 3.4

Circuit Breakers	Breaking Capacity (kA)	
BS 3871 Types 1, 2, 3, etc.	1	(M1)
	1.5	(M1.5)
	3	(M3)
	4.5	(M4.5)
	6	(M6)
	9	(M9)
BS EN 60898 Types B, C, D	I_{cn} 1.5	I_{cs} 1.5
	3	3
	6	6
	10	7.5
	15	7.5
	25	10

*I_{cn} is the rated ultimate breaking capacity. I_{cs} is the maximum
breaking capacity operation after which the breaker may still be used
without loss of performance.*

Fuse and circuit breaker operation

Let us consider a protective device rated at, say, 10 A. This value
of current can be carried indefinitely by the device, and is known
as its nominal setting I_n. The value of the current which will
cause operation of the device, I_2, will be larger than I_n, and will
be dependent on the device's *fusing factor*. This is a figure which,
when multiplied by the nominal setting I_n, will indicate the value
of operating current I_2.

For fuses to BS 88 and BS 1361 and circuit breakers to BS 3871
this fusing factor is approximately 1.45; hence our 10 A device
would not operate until the current reached 1.45 × 10 = 14.5 A.

The IEE Regulations require coordination between conductors and
protection when an overload occurs, such that:

1. The nominal setting of the device I_n is greater than or equal
   to the design current of the circuit I_b ($I_n \geqslant I_b$).

Table 3.5   British Standards for Fuse Links.

Standard		Current Rating	Voltage Rating
1	BS 2950	Range 0.05–25 A	Range 1000 V (0.05 A) to 32 V (25 A) AC and DC
2	BS 646	1, 2, 3 and 5 A	Up to 250 V AC and DC
3	BS 1362 cartridge	1, 2, 3, 5, 7, 10 and 13 A	Up to 250 V AC
4	BS 1361 HRC cut-out fuses	5, 15, 20, 30, 45 and 60 A	Up to 250 V AC
5	BS 88 motors	Four ranges, 2–1200 A	Up to 660 V, but normally 250 or 415 V AC and 250 or 500 V DC
6	BS 2692	Main range from 5 to 200 A; 0.5 to 3 A for voltage transformer protective fuses	Range from 2.2 to 132 kV
7	BS 3036 rewirable	5, 15, 20, 30, 45, 60, 100, 150 and 200 A	Up to 250 V to earth
8	BS 4265	500 mA to 6.3 A, 32 mA to 2 A	Up to 250 V AC

Breaking Capacity	Notes
1. Two or three times current rating	Cartridge fuse links for telecommunication and light electrical apparatus. Very low breaking capacity
2. 1000 A	Cartridge fuse intended for fused plugs and adapters to BS 546: 'round-pin' plugs
3. 6000 A	Cartridge fuse primarily intended for BS 1363: 'flat-pin' plugs
4. 16 500 A, 33 000 A	Cartridge fuse intended for use in domestic consumer units. The dimensions prevent interchangeability of fuse links which are not of the same current rating
5. Ranges from 10 000 to 80 000 A in four AC and three DC categories	Part 1 of Standard gives performance and dimensions of cartridge fuse links, whilst Part 2 gives performance and requirements of fuse carriers and fuse bases designed to accommodate fuse links complying with Part 1
6. Ranges from 25 to 750 MVA (main range), 50 to 2500 MVA (VT fuses)	Fuses for AC power circuits above 660 V
7. Ranges from 1000 to 12 000 A	Semi-enclosed fuses (the element is a replacement wire) for AC and DC circuits
8. 1500 A (high breaking capacity), 35 A (low breaking capacity)	Miniature fuse links for protection of appliances of up to 250 V (metric standard)

2. The nominal setting I_n is less than or equal to the lowest current-carrying capacity I_z of any of the circuit conductors $(I_n \leqslant I_z)$.
3. The operating current of the device I_2 is less than or equal to $1.45\,I_z$ $(I_2 \leqslant 1.45\,I_z)$.

So, for our 10 A device, if the cable is rated at 10 A then condition 2 is satisfied. Since the fusing factor is 1.45, condition 3 is also satisfied: $I_2 = I_n \times 1.45 = 10 \times 1.45$, which is also 1.45 times the 10 A cable rating.

The problem arises when a BS 3036 semi-enclosed rewirable fuse is used, as it may have a fusing factor of as much as 2. In order to comply with condition 3, I_n should be less than or equal to $0.725\,I_z$.

This figure is derived from $1.45/2 = 0.725$. For example, if a cable is rated at 10 A, then I_n for a BS 3036 should be $0.725 \times 10 = 7.25$ A. As the fusing factor is 2, the operating current $I_2 = 2 \times 7.25 = 14.5$, which conforms with condition 3, i.e. $I_2 \leqslant 1.45 \times 10 = 14.5$.

All of these foregoing requirements ensure that conductor insulation is undamaged when an overload occurs.

Under fault conditions it is the conductor itself that is susceptible to damage and must be protected. Figure 3.4 shows one half-cycle of short-circuit current if there were no protection. The RMS value $(0.7071 \times \text{maximum value})$ is called the PFC. The cut-off point is where the fault current is interrupted and an arc is formed; the time t_1 taken to reach this point is called the pre-arcing time. After the current has been cut off, it falls to zero as the arc is being extinguished. The time t_2 is the total time taken to disconnect the fault.

During the time t_1, the protective device is allowing energy to pass through to the load side of the circuit. This energy is known as the

Short-circuit current (amperes)

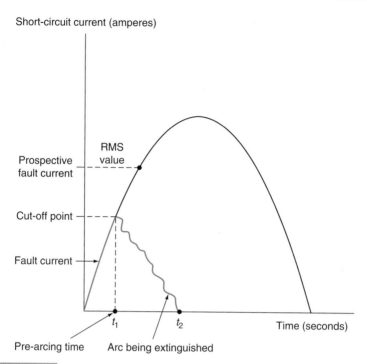

FIGURE 3.4 Let-through energy.

pre-arcing let-through energy and is given by $I^2 t_1$, where I is the fault current. The total let-through energy from start to disconnection of the fault is given by $I^2 t_2$ (see Figure 3.5 and Table 3.6).

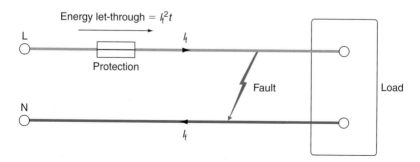

FIGURE 3.5 Let-through energy.

For faults of up to 5 s duration, the amount of heat energy that cable can withstand is given by k^2s^2, where s is the cross-sectional area of the conductor and k is a factor dependent on the conduct or material. Hence, the let-through energy should not exceed k^2s^2, i.e. $I^2t = k^2s^2$. If we transpose this formula for t, we get $t = k^2s^2/I^2$, which is the maximum disconnection time in seconds.

Remember that these requirements refer to fault currents only. If, in fact, the protective device has been selected to protect against overloads and has a breaking capacity not less than the PFC at the point of installation, it will also protect against fault currents. However, if there is any doubt the formula should be used.

For example, in Figure 3.6, if I_n has been selected for overload protection, the questions to be asked are as follows:

1. Is $I_n \geqslant I_b$?   Yes
2. Is $I_n \leqslant I_z$?   Yes
3. Is $I_2 \geqslant 1.45 I_z$?   Yes

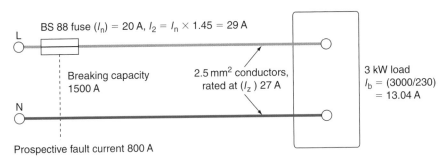

BS 88 fuse (I_n) = 20 A, $I_2 = I_n \times 1.45 = 29$ A

Breaking capacity 1500 A

2.5 mm^2 conductors, rated at (I_z) 27 A

3 kW load
I_b = (3000/230) = 13.04 A

Prospective fault current 800 A

FIGURE 3.6

Then, if the device has a rated breaking capacity not less than the PFC, it can be considered to give protection against fault current also.

When an installation is being designed, the PFC at every relevant point must be determined, by either calculation or measurement. The value will decrease as we move farther away from the intake position (resistance increases with length). Thus, if the breaking

Table 3.6 I^2t characteristics: 2–800 A Fuse Links. Discrimination is Achieved if the Total I^2t of the Minor Fuse Does Not Exceed the Pre-arcing I^2t of the Major Fuse.

Rating (A)	I^2t Pre-arcing	I^2t Total at 400 V
2	0.9	17
4	4	12
6	16	59
10	56	170
16	190	580
20	310	810
25	630	1700
32	1200	2800
40	2000	6000
50	3600	11000
63	6500	14000
80	13000	36000
100	24 000	66000
125	34 000	120000
160	80 000	260000
200	140 000	400000
250	230 000	560000
315	360000	920000
350	550000	1300000
400	800 000	2300000
450	700000	1400000
500	900 000	1800000
630	2200000	4500000
700	2500 000	5000000
800	4300 000	10000000

capacity of the lowest rated fuse in the installation is greater than the PFC at the origin of the supply, there is no need to determine the value except at the origin.

Discrimination (IEE Regulation 536.2)

When we discriminate, we indicate our preference over other choices: this house rather than that house, for example. With protection we have to ensure that the correct device operates when there is a fault. Hence, a 13A BS 1362 plug fuse should operate before the main circuit fuse. Logically, protection starts at the origin of an installation with a large device and progresses down the chain with smaller and smaller sizes.

Simply because protective devices have different ratings, it cannot be assumed that discrimination is achieved. This is especially the case where a mixture of different types of device is used. However, as a general rule a 2:1 ratio with the lower-rated devices will be satisfactory. The table on page 67 shows how fuse links may be chosen to ensure discrimination.

Fuses will give discrimination if the figure in column 3 does not exceed the figure in column 2. Hence:

a 2A fuse will discriminate with a 4A fuse
a 4A fuse will discriminate with a 6A fuse
a 6A fuse will *not* discriminate with a 10A fuse
a 10A fuse will discriminate with a 16A fuse.

All other fuses will *not* discriminate with the next highest fuse, and in some cases several sizes higher are needed, e.g. a 250A fuse will only discriminate with a 400A fuse.

Position of protective devices (IEE Regulations 433.2 and 434.2)

When there is a reduction in the current-carrying capacity of a conductor, a protective device is required. There are, however, some exceptions to this requirement; these are listed quite clearly in Sections 433 and 434 of the IEE Regulations. As an example, protection is not needed in a ceiling rose where the cable size changes from 1.0mm^2 to, say, 0.5mm^2 for the lampholder flex. This is permitted as it is not expected that lamps will cause overloads.

PROTECTION AGAINST OVERVOLTAGE (IEE REGULATIONS SECTION 443)

This chapter deals with the requirements of an electrical installation to withstand overvoltages caused by lightning or switching surges. It is unlikely that installations in the UK will be affected by the requirements of this section as the number of thunderstorm days per year is not likely to exceed 25.

PROTECTION AGAINST UNDERVOLTAGE (IEE REGULATIONS SECTION 445)

From the point of view of danger in the event of a drop or loss of voltage, the protection should prevent automatic restarting of machinery, etc. In fact, such protection is an integral part of motor starters in the form of the control circuit.

CHAPTER 4

Isolation Switching and Control

DEFINITIONS USED IN THIS CHAPTER

Emergency switching Rapid cutting off of electrical energy to remove any hazard to persons, livestock or property which may occur unexpectedly.

Isolation Cutting off an electrical installation, a circuit or an item of equipment from every source of electrical energy.

Mechanical maintenance The replacement, refurbishment or cleaning of lamps and non-electrical parts of equipment, plant and machinery.

Switch A mechanical switching device capable of making, carrying and breaking current under normal circuit conditions, which may include specified overload conditions, and also of carrying, for a specified time, currents under specified abnormal conditions such as those of short circuit.

ISOLATION AND SWITCHING (IEE REGULATIONS SECTION 537)

All installations, whether they be the whole or part, must have a means of isolation and switching for various reasons. These are:

1. To remove possible dangers associated with the installation/operation/testing of electrical installations.
2. To provide a means of functional switching and control.

The IEE Regulations make reference to:

1. **Switching off for mechanical maintenance** The devices for this function should be manually operated and preferably located in the main supply circuit.
2. **Emergency switching** The devices for this function should preferably be hand operated and be capable of interrupting the full load of the circuit concerned.
3. **Functional switching** This is simply switching an item on or off to control its function, e.g. a light switch.
4. **Firefighters' switches** Clearly for the function of isolation in the event of a fire. They should be coloured red and be installed no more than 2.75 m above the ground with the OFF position at the top.

The following chart (Table 4.1) shows type and uses of various devices used for isolation and switching.

Table 4.1   Selection of Generally Used Devices.

Device	Isolation	Emergency	Function
Circuit breakers	Yes	Yes	Yes
RCDs	Yes	Yes	Yes
Isolating switches	Yes	Yes	Yes
Plugs and socket outlets	Yes	No	Yes
Ditto but over 32 A	Yes	No	No
Switched fused connection unit	Yes	Yes	Yes
Unswitched fused connection unit	Yes	No	No
Plug fuses	Yes	No	No
Cooker units	Yes	Yes	Yes

Control

Motor control

This is usually part of the motor starter and most importantly must prevent automatic restarting after loss of supply and subsequent restoration, i.e undervoltage protection.

CHAPTER 5

Circuit Design

DEFINITIONS USED IN THIS CHAPTER

Ambient temperature The temperature of the air or other medium where the equipment is to be used.

Circuit protective conductor A protective conductor connecting exposed conductive parts of equipment to the main earthing terminal.

Current-carrying capacity The maximum current which can be carried by a conductor under specified conditions without its steady state temperature exceeding a specified value.

Design current The magnitude of the current intended to be carried by a circuit in normal service.

Earthing conductor A protective conductor connecting a main earthing terminal of an installation to an earth electrode or other means of earthing.

Fault current An overcurrent resulting from a fault of negligible impedance between live conductors (short-circuit current) or between a line conductor and earth (earth fault current).

Overcurrent A current exceeding the rated value. For conductors the rated value is the current-carrying capacity.

DESIGN PROCEDURE

The requirements of IEE Regulations make it clear that circuits must be designed and the design data made readily available. In fact, this has always been the case with previous editions of the Regulations, but it has not been so clearly indicated.

How then do we begin to design? Clearly, plunging into calculations of cable size is of little value unless the type of cable and its method of installation are known. This, in turn, will depend on the installation's environment. At the same time, we would need to know whether the supply was single- or three-phase, the type of earthing arrangements, and so on. Here then is our starting point and it is referred to in the Regulations, Chapter 3, as 'Assessment of general characteristics'.

Having ascertained all the necessary details, we can decide on an installation method, the type of cable, and how we will protect against electric shock and overcurrents. We would now be ready to begin the calculation part of the design procedure.

Basically there are eight stages in such a procedure. These are the same whatever the type of installation, be it a cooker circuit or a distribution cable feeding a distribution board in a factory. Here, then, are the eight basic steps in a simplified form:

1. Determine the design current I_b.
2. Select the rating of the protection I_n.
3. Select the relevant rating factors (CFs).
4. Divide I_n by the relevant CFs to give tabulated cable current-carrying capacity I_t.
5. Choose a cable size, to suit I_t.
6. Check the voltage drop.
7. Check for shock risk constraints.
8. Check for thermal constraints.

Let us now examine each stage in detail.

Add to this the requirement to select conduit and trunking sizes and we have a complete design.

DESIGN CURRENT

In many instances the design current I_b is quoted by the manufacturer, but there are times when it has to be calculated. In that case there are two formulae involved, one for single-phase and one for three-phase:

Single-phase:

$$I_b = \frac{P \text{ (watts)}}{V} \quad (V \text{ usually } 230 \text{ V})$$

Three-phase:

$$I_b = \frac{P \text{ (watts)}}{\sqrt{3} \times V_L} \quad (V_L \text{ usually } 400 \text{ V})$$

Current is in amperes, and power P in watts.

If an item of equipment has a power factor (PF) and/or has moving parts, efficiency (eff) will have to be taken into account.

Hence:

Single-phase:

$$I_b = \frac{P \text{ (watts)} \times 100}{V \times PF \times eff}$$

Three-phase:

$$I_b = \frac{P \times 100}{\sqrt{3} \times V_L \times PF \times eff}$$

NOMINAL SETTING OF PROTECTION

Having determined I_b we must now select the nominal setting of the protection such that $I_n \geqslant I_b$. This value may be taken from IEE Regulations, Tables 41.2, 41.3 or 41.4 or from manufacturers' charts. The choice of fuse or CB type is also important and may have to be changed if cable sizes or loop impedances are too high. These details will be discussed later.

Rating factors

When a cable carries its full load current it can become warm. This is no problem unless its temperature rises further due to other influences, in which case the insulation could be damaged by overheating. These other influences are: high ambient temperature; cables grouped together closely; uncleared overcurrents; and contact with thermal insulation.

For each of these conditions there is a rating factor (CF) which will respectively be called C_a, C_g, C_c and C_i, and which de-rates cable current-carrying capacity or conversely increases cable size.

Ambient temperature C$_a$

The cable ratings in the IEE Regulations are based on an ambient temperature of 30°C, and hence it is only above this temperature that an adverse correction is needed. Table 4B1 of the Regulations gives factors for all types of insulation.

Grouping C$_g$

When cables are grouped together they impart heat to each other. Therefore, the more cables there are the more heat they will generate, thus increasing the temperature of each cable. Table 4C1 of the Regulations gives factors for such groups of cables or circuits. It should be noted that the figures given are for uniform groups of cables equally loaded, and hence correction may not necessarily be needed for cables grouped at the outlet of a domestic consumer unit, for example where there is a mixture of different sizes.

A typical situation where rating factors need to be applied would be in the calculation of cable sizes for a lighting system in a large factory. Here many cables of the same size and loading may be grouped together in trunking and could be expected to be fully loaded all at the same time.

Protection by BS 3036 fuse and/or when the cable is underground C_c

As we have already discussed in Chapter 3, because of the high fusing factor of BS 3036 fuses, the rating of the fuse I_n should be $\leqslant 0.725\, I_z$.

Hence 0.725 is the rating factor to be used when BS 3036 fuses are used.

If the cable is in a duct underground or buried direct the factor is 0.9.

If both conditions exist the factor is $0.725 \times 0.9 = 0.653$.

Thermal insulation C_i

With the modern trend towards energy saving and the installation of thermal insulation, there may be a need to de-rate cables to account for heat retention.

The values of cable current-carrying capacity given in Appendix 4 of the IEE Regulations have been adjusted for situations when thermal insulation touches one side of a cable. However, if a cable is totally surrounded by thermal insulation for more than 0.5 m, a factor of 0.5 must be applied to the tabulated clipped direct ratings. For less than 0.5 m, de-rating factors (Table 52.2 of the Regulations) should be applied.

Application of rating factors

Some or all of the onerous conditions just outlined may affect a cable along its whole length or parts of it, but not all may affect it at the same time. So, consider the following:

1. If the cable in Figure 5.1 ran for the whole of its length, grouped with others of the same size in a high ambient temperature, and was totally surrounded with thermal insulation, it would seem logical to apply all the CFs, as they all affect the whole cable run. Certainly the factors for the BS 3036 fuse, grouping and thermal insulation should be used. However, it is doubtful if the ambient temperature will have any effect on the cable, as the thermal insulation, if it is efficient, will prevent heat reaching the cable. Hence, apply C_g, C_c and C_i.

2. In Figure 5.2a the cable first runs grouped, then leaves the group and runs in high ambient temperature, and finally is enclosed in thermal insulation. We therefore have three different conditions, each affecting the cable in different areas. The BS 3036 fuse affects the whole cable run and therefore C_c must be used, but there is no need to apply all of the remaining factors as the worse one will automatically compensate for the others. The relevant factors are shown in Figure 5.2b; apply only $C_c = 0.725$ and $C_i = 0.5$. If protection was *not* by BS 3036 fuse, then apply only $C_i = 0.5$.

3. In Figure 5.3a combination of cases 1 and 2 is considered. The effect of grouping and ambient temperature is $0.7 \times 0.97 = 0.69$. The factor for thermal insulation is still worse than this combination, and therefore C_i is the only one to be used.

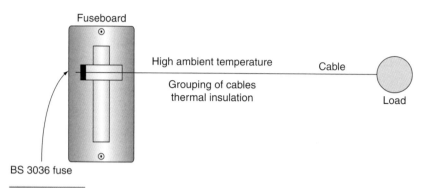

FIGURE 5.1

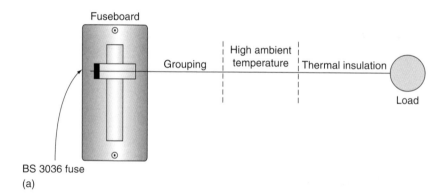

BS 3036 fuse
(a)

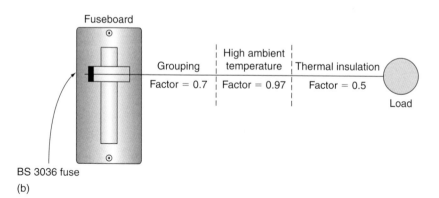

BS 3036 fuse
(b)

FIGURE 5.2

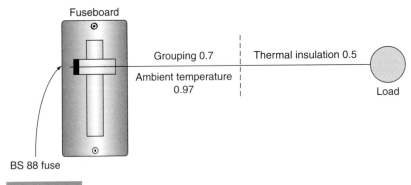

Fuseboard

Grouping 0.7

Thermal insulation 0.5

Ambient temperature 0.97

Load

BS 88 fuse

FIGURE 5.3

Having chosen the *relevant* rating factors, we now apply them to the nominal rating of the protection I_n as divisors in order to calculate the current-carrying capacity I_t of the cable.

Tabulated current-carrying capacity

The required formula for current-carrying capacity I_t is:

$$I_t \geq I_n$$

relevant CFs

In Figure 5.4 the current-carrying capacity is given by

$$I_t \geq \frac{I_n}{C_c C_i} = \frac{30}{0.725 \times 0.5} = 82.75 \text{ A}$$

or, without the BS 3036 fuse:

$$I_t \geq \frac{30}{0.5} = 60 \text{ A}$$

In Figure 5.4, $C_a C_i = 0.97 \times 0.5 = 0.485$, which is worse than C_i (0.5) (Figure 5.5).

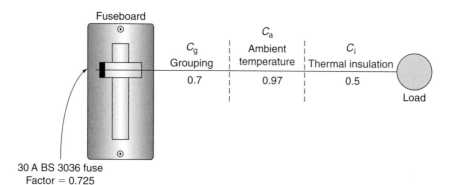

Fuseboard

C_g Grouping 0.7

C_a Ambient temperature 0.97

C_i Thermal insulation 0.5

Load

30 A BS 3036 fuse
Factor = 0.725

FIGURE 5.4

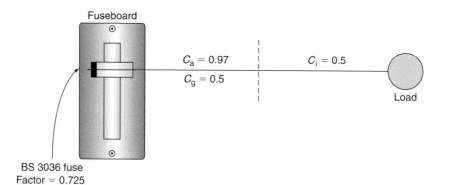

Fuseboard

$C_a = 0.97$
$C_g = 0.5$

$C_i = 0.5$

Load

BS 3036 fuse
Factor = 0.725

FIGURE 5.5

Hence:

$$I_t \geq \frac{I_n}{C_c C_a C_g} = \frac{30}{0.725 \times 0.485} = 85.3 \, \text{A}$$

or, without the BS 3036 fuse:

$$I_t = \frac{30}{0.485} = 61.85 \, \text{A}$$

Note: If the circuit is not subject to overload, I_n can be replaced by I_b so the formula becomes:

$$I_t \geq \frac{I_b}{\text{CFs}}$$

Choice of cable size

Having established the tabulated current-carrying capacity I_t of the cable to be used, it now remains to choose a cable to suit that value. The tables in Appendix 4 of the IEE Regulations list all the cable sizes, current-carrying capacities and voltage drops of the various types of cable. For example, for PVC-insulated singles, single-phase, in conduit, having a current-carrying capacity of 45 A, the installation is by reference method B (Table 4A2), the cable table is 4D1A and the column is 4. Hence, the cable size is 10.0 mm² (column 1).

VOLTAGE DROP (IEE REGULATIONS 525 AND APPENDIX 12)

The resistance of a conductor increases as the length increases and/or the cross-sectional area decreases. Associated with an increased resistance is a drop in voltage, which means that a load at the end of a long thin cable will not have the full supply voltage available (Figure 5.6).

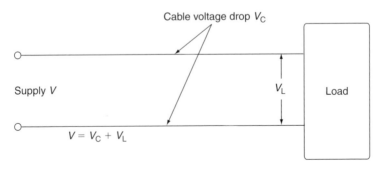

FIGURE 5.6 Voltage drop.

The IEE Regulations require that the voltage drop V should not be so excessive that equipment does not function safely. They further indicate that the following percentages of the nominal voltage at the *origin* of the circuit will satisfy. This means that:

	LV Lighting (3%)	LV Power (5%)
230 V single-phase	6.9 V	11.5 V
400 V three-phase	12 V	20 V

For example, the voltage drop on a power circuit supplied from a 230 V source by a $16.0\,mm^2$ two-core copper cable 23 m long, clipped direct and carrying a design current of 33 A, will be:

$$V_c = \frac{mV \times I_b \times L}{1000} \text{ (mV; from Table 4D2B)}$$

$$= \frac{28 \times 33 \times 23}{1000} = 21.25\text{ V}$$

As we know that the maximum voltage drop in this instance (230 V) is 11.5 V, we can determine the maximum length by transposing the formula:

$$\text{maximum length} = \frac{V_c \times 1000}{mV \times I_b}$$

$$= \frac{11.5 \times 1000}{28 \times 23} = 17.8\text{ m}$$

There are other constraints, however, which may not permit such a length.

SHOCK RISK (IEE REGULATIONS SECTION 411)

This topic has already been discussed in full in Chapter 2. To recap, however, the actual loop impedance Z_s should not exceed those values given in Tables 41.2, 41.3 and 41.4 of the IEE Regulations. This ensures that circuits feeding final and distribution circuits will be disconnected, in the event of an earth fault, in the required time.

Remember $Z_s = Z_e + R_1 + R_2$.

THERMAL CONSTRAINTS (IEE REGULATIONS SECTION 543)

The IEE Regulations require that we either select or check the size of a cpc against Table 54.7 of the Regulations, or calculate its size using an adiabatic equation.

Selection of cpc using Table 54.7

Table 54.7 of the Regulations simply tells us that:

1. For line conductors up to and including 16 mm², the cpc should be at least the same size.
2. For sizes between 16 mm² and 35 mm², the cpc should be at least 16 mm².
3. For sizes of line conductor over 35 mm², the cpc should be at least half this size.

This is all very well, but for large sizes of line conductor the cpc is also large and hence costly to supply and install. Also, composite cables such as the typical twin with cpc 6242Y type have cpcs smaller than the line conductor and hence do not comply with Table 54.7.

Calculation of cpc using an adiabatic equation

The adiabatic equation

$$s = \frac{\sqrt{I^2 t}}{k}$$

enables us to check on a selected size of cable, or on an actual size in a multicore cable. In order to apply the equation we need first to calculate the earth fault current from:

$$I = U_0/Z_s$$

where U_0 is the nominal line voltage to earth (usually 230V) and Z_s is the actual earth fault loop impedance. Next we select a k factor from Tables 54.2 to 54.7 of the Regulations, and then determine the disconnection time t from the relevant curve.

For those unfamiliar with such curves, using them may appear a daunting task. A brief explanation may help to dispel any fears. Referring to any of the curves for fuses in Appendix 3 of the IEE Regulations, we can see that the current scale goes from 1A to 10 000A, and the time scale from 0.01s to 10 000s. One can imagine the difficulty in drawing a scale between 1A and 10 000A in divisions of 1A, and so a logarithmic scale is used. This cramps the large scale into a small area. All the subdivisions between the major divisions increase in equal amounts depending on the major division boundaries; for example, all the subdivisions between 100 and 1000 are in amounts of 100 (Figure 5.7).

Figures 5.8 and 5.9 give the IEE Regulations time/current curves for BS 88 fuses. Referring to the appropriate curve for a 32A fuse (Figure 5.9), we find that a fault current of 200A will cause disconnection of the supply in 0.6s.

Where a value falls between two subdivisions, for example 150A, an estimate of its position must be made. Remember that even if the scale is not visible, it would be cramped at one end; so 150A would not fall half-way between 100A and 200A (Figure 5.8).

It will be noted in Appendix 3 of the Regulations that each set of curves is accompanied by a table which indicates the current that

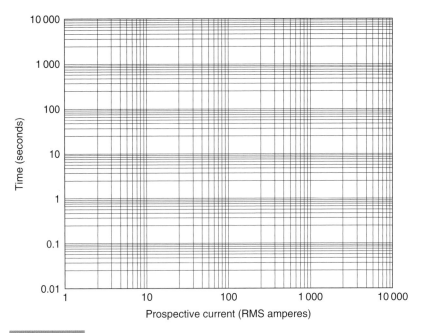

FIGURE 5.7

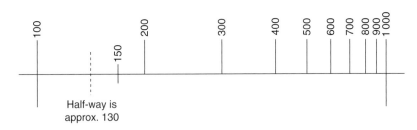

FIGURE 5.8

causes operation of the protective device for disconnection times of 0.1 s, 0.4 s and 5 s.

The IEE Regulations curves for CBs to BS EN 60898 type B and RCBOs are shown in Figure 5.9.

Having found a disconnection time, we can now apply the formula.

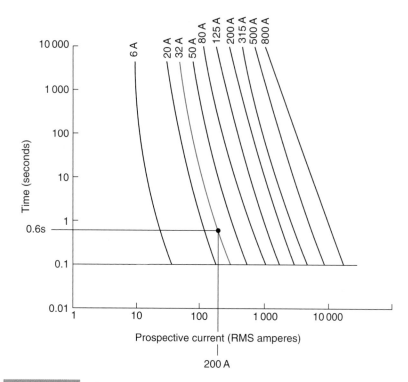

FIGURE 5.9 Time/current characteristics for fuses to BS 88 Part 2. Example for 32 A fuse superimposed.

EXAMPLE OF USE OF THE ADIABATIC EQUATION

Suppose that in a design the protection was by 40 A BS 88 fuse; we had chosen a 4.0 mm² copper cpc running with our line conductor; and the loop impedance Z_s was 1.15 Ω. Would the chosen cpc size be large enough to withstand damage in the event of an earth fault? We have:

$$I = U_0/Z_s = 230/1.15 = 200 \text{ A}$$

From the appropriate curve for the 40 A BS 88 fuse (Figure 5.10), we obtain a disconnection time t of 2 s. From Table 54.3 of

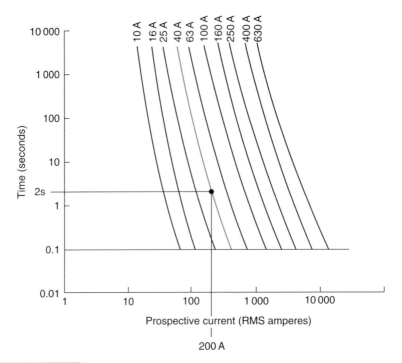

FIGURE 5.10 Time/current characteristics for fuses to BS 88 Part 2. Example for 40 A fuse superimposed.

the Regulations, $k = 115$. Therefore the minimum size of cpc is given by:

$$s = \frac{\sqrt{I^2 t}}{k} = \frac{\sqrt{200^2 \times 2}}{115} = 2.46\,\text{mm}^2$$

So our 4.0 mm² cpc is acceptable. Beware of thinking that the answer means that we could change the 4.0 mm² for a 2.5 mm². If we did, the loop impedance would be different and hence I and t would change; the answer for s would probably tell us to use a 4.0 mm².

In the example shown, 's' is merely a check on the actual size chosen.

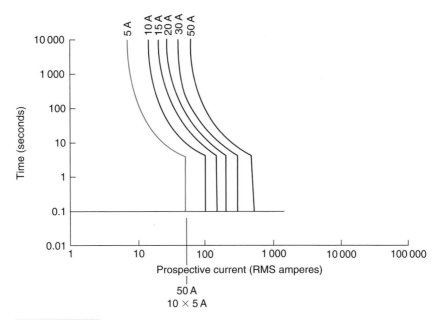

FIGURE 5.11 Time/current characteristics for type 3 CBs to BS EN 60898 and RCBOs. Example for 50 A superimposed. For times less than 20 ms, the manufacturer should be consulted.

Installation methods (IEE Regulations Table 4.2)

Figures 5.12–5.18 illustrate some of the common methods of cable installation.

Having discussed each component of the design procedure, we can now put them all together to form a complete design.

AN EXAMPLE OF CIRCUIT DESIGN

A consumer lives in a bungalow with a detached garage and work-shop, as shown in Figure 5.19 (see page 94). The building method is traditional brick and timber.

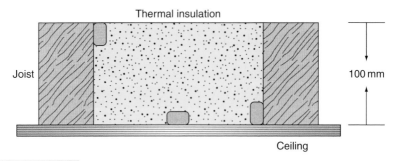

FIGURE 5.12 Method 100.

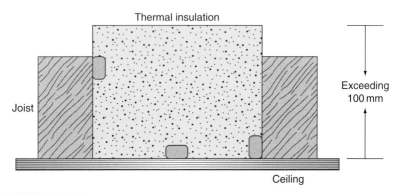

FIGURE 5.13 Method 101.

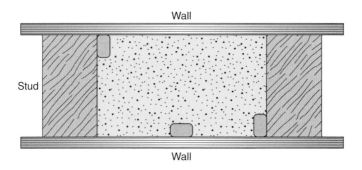

FIGURE 5.14 Method 102.

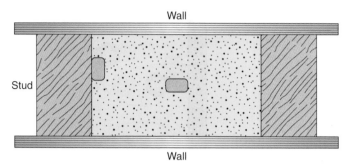

FIGURE 5.15   Method 103.

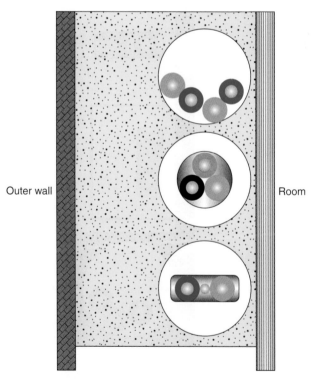

FIGURE 5.16   Method A.

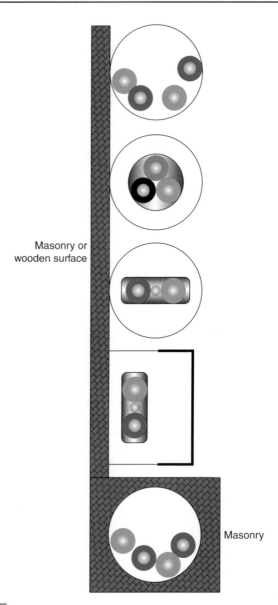

FIGURE 5.17   Method B.

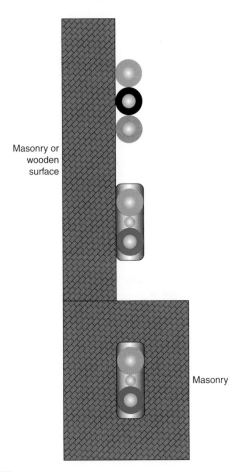

Masonry or
wooden
surface

Masonry

FIGURE 5.18 Method C.

The mains intake position is at high level and comprises an 80 A
BS 1361 230 V main fuse, an 80 A rated meter and a six-way 80 A
consumer unit housing BS EN 60898 Type B CBs as follows:

Ring circuit	32 A
Lighting circuit	6 A
Immersion heater circuit	16 A
Cooker circuit	32 A
Shower circuit	32 A
Spare way	–

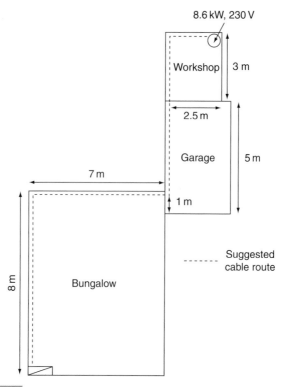

FIGURE 5.19

The cooker is rated at 30 A, with no socket in the cooker unit. The main tails are 16.0 mm² double-insulated PVC, with a 6.0 mm² earthing conductor. There is no main protective bonding. The earthing system is TN-S, with an external loop impedance Z_e of 0.3 ohms. The prospective short-circuit current (PSCC) at the origin has been measured as 800 A. The roof space is insulated to full depth of the ceiling joists and the temperature in the roof space is not expected to exceed over 35 °C.

The consumer wishes to convert the workshop into a pottery room and install an 8.6 kW/230 V electric kiln. The design procedure is as follows.

ASSESSMENT OF GENERAL CHARACTERISTICS

The present maximum demand, applying diversity, is:

Ring	32 A
Lighting (66% of 6 A)	3.96 A
Immersion heater	16 A
Cooker (10 A + 30% of 20 A)	16 A
Shower	32 A
Total	**100 A**

Reference to the current rating tables in the IEE Regulations will show that the existing main tails are too small and should be up-rated. So, the addition of another 8.6 kW of load is not possible with the present arrangement.

The current taken by the kiln is $8600/230 = 37.4$ A. Therefore, the new maximum demand is $100 + 37.4 = 137.4$ A.

Supply details are:
single-phase 230 V, 50 Hz earthing; TN-S PSCC at origin (measured): 800 A.

Decisions must now be made as to the type of cable, the installation method and the type of protective device. As the existing arrangement is not satisfactory, the supply authority must be informed of the new maximum demand, as a larger main fuse and service cable may be required.

SIZING THE MAIN TAILS

1. The new load on the existing consumer unit will be 137.4 A. From the IEE Regulations, the cable size is 25.0 mm².
2. The earthing conductor size, from the IEE Regulations, will be 16.0 mm². The main equipotential bonding conductor size, from the IEE Regulations, will be 10.0 mm².

For a domestic installation such as this, a PVC flat twin cable, clipped direct (avoiding any thermal insulation) through the loft space and the garage, etc., would be most appropriate.

SIZING THE KILN CIRCUIT CABLE

Design current I_b is

$$I_b = \frac{P}{V} = \frac{8600}{230} = 37.4 \text{ A}$$

Rating and type of protection I_n
As we have seen, the requirement for the rating I_n is that $I_n \geqslant I_b$. Therefore, using the tables in the IEE Regulations, I_n will be 40 A.

Correction factors:

C_a: 0.94
C_g: not applicable
C_c: 0.725 **only** if the fuse is BS 3036 (not applicable here)
C_i: 0.5 if the cable is totally surrounded in thermal insulation (not applicable here).

Tabulated current-carrying capacity of cable

$$I_t = \frac{I_n}{CF} = \frac{40}{0.94} = 42.5 \text{ A}$$

Cable size based on tabulated current-carrying capacity

Table 4D5A IEE Regulations give a size of 6.0 mm^2 for this value of I_t (method C).

Check on voltage drop

The actual voltage drop is given by

$$\frac{mV \times I_b \times 1}{1000} = \frac{7.3 \times 37.4 \times 24.5}{1000} = 6.7\,V$$

(well below the
maximum of $11.5\,V$)

This voltage drop, whilst not causing the kiln to work unsafely, may mean inefficiency, and it is perhaps better to use a $10.0\,mm^2$ cable.

For a $10.0\,mm^2$ cable, the voltage drop is checked as

$$\frac{4.4 \times 37.4 \times 24.5}{1000} = 4.04\,V$$

Shock risk

The cpc associated with a $10.0\,mm^2$ twin 6242 Y cable is $4.0\,mm^2$. Hence, the total loop impedance will be

$$Z_s = Z_e + \frac{(R_1 + R_2) \times L \times 1.2}{1000}$$
$$= 0.3 + \frac{6.44 \times 24.5 \times 1.2}{1000} = 0.489\,\Omega$$

Note

6.44 is the tabulated $(R_1 + R_2)$ value and the multiplier 1.2 takes account of the conductor resistance at its operating temperature.

It is likely that the chosen CB will be a type B.

Thermal constraints

We still need to check that the $4.0\,\text{mm}^2$ cpc is large enough to withstand damage under earth fault conditions. So, the fault current would be

$$I = \frac{U_0}{Z_\text{s}} = \frac{230}{0.489} = 470\,\text{A}$$

The disconnection time t for this current for this type of protection (from the relevant curve in the IEE Regulations) is as follows.

$40\,\text{A}$ CB type B $= 0.1\,\text{s}$ (the actual time is less than this but $0.1\,\text{s}$ is the instantaneous time).

From the regulations, the factor for $k = 115$. We can now apply the adiabatic equation

$$S = \frac{\sqrt{I^2 \times t}}{k} = \frac{\sqrt{470^2 \times 0.1}}{115} = 1.29\,\text{mm}^2$$

Hence, our $4.0\,\text{mm}^2$ cpc is of adequate size.

Summary

The kiln circuit would be protected by a $40\,\text{A}$ BS EN 60898 type B CB and supplied from a spare way in the consumer unit. The main fuse would need to be up-rated to $100\,\text{A}$. The main tails would be changed to $25.0\,\text{mm}^2$. The earthing conductor would be changed to $16.0\,\text{mm}^2$.

Main protective bonding conductors would need to be installed $10.0\,\text{mm}^2$ twin with earth PVC cable.

CHAPTER 6

Inspection and Testing

DEFINITIONS USED IN THIS CHAPTER

Earth electrode A conductor or group of conductors in intimate contact with and providing an electrical connection with earth.

Earth fault loop impedance The impedance of the earth fault loop (line-to-earth loop) starting and ending at the point of earth fault.

Residual current device (RCD) An electromechanical switching device or association of devices intended to cause the opening of the contacts when the residual current attains a given value under specified conditions.

Ring final circuit A final circuit arranged in the form of a ring and connected to a single point of supply.

TESTING SEQUENCE (PART 7)

Having designed our installation, selected the appropriate materials and equipment, and installed the system, it now remains to put it into service. However, before this happens, the installation must be tested and inspected to ensure that it complies, as far as is practicable, with the IEE Regulations. Note the word 'practicable'; it would be unreasonable, for example, to expect the whole length of a circuit cable to be inspected for defects, as this may mean lifting floorboards, etc.

Part 6 of the IEE Regulations gives details of testing and inspection requirements. Unfortunately, these requirements pre-suppose that the person carrying out the testing is in possession of all the design data, which is only likely to be the case on the larger commercial or industrial projects. It may be wise for the person who will eventually sign the test certificate to indicate that the test and inspection were carried out as far as was possible in the absence of any design or other information.

However, let us continue by examining the required procedures. The Regulations initially call for a visual inspection, but some items such as correct connection of conductors, etc. can be done during the actual testing. A preferred sequence of tests is recommended, where relevant, and is as follows:

1. Continuity of protective conductors
2. Continuity of ring final circuit conductors
3. Insulation resistance
4. Protection by SELV or PELV or electrical separation
5. Protection by barriers and enclosures provided during erection
6. Insulation of non-conducting floors and walls
7. Polarity
8. Earth electrode resistance
9. Earth fault loop impedance
10. Additional protection
11. Prospective fault current (PFC)
12. Check of phase sequence
13. Functional testing
14. Verification of voltage drop.

Not all of the tests may be relevant, of course. For example, in a domestic installation (TN-S or TN-C-S) only tests 1, 2, 3, 7, 9, 10, 11 and 13 would be needed.

The Regulations indicate quite clearly the tests required in Part 6. Let us then take a closer look at some of them in order to understand the reasoning behind them.

Continuity of protective conductors

All protective conductors, including main protective and supplementary bonding conductors, must be tested for continuity using a low-reading ohmmeter.

For main protective bonding conductors there is no single fixed value of resistance above which the conductor would be deemed unsuitable. Each measured value, if indeed it is measurable for very short lengths, should be compared with the relevant value for a particular conductor length and size. Such values are shown in Table 6.1.

Table 6.1

Conductor Size (mm²)	Resistance (mΩ/m)
1.0	18.1
1.5	12.1
2.5	7.41
4.0	4.61
6.0	3.08
10.0	1.83
16.0	1.15
25.0	0.727
35.0	0.524

Where a supplementary protective bonding conductor has been installed between *simultaneously accessible* exposed and extraneous conductive parts, because circuit disconnection times cannot be met, then the resistance R of the conductor must be equal to or less than $50/I_a$. So:

$$R \leq 50/I_a \; \Omega$$

where 50 is the voltage, above which exposed metalwork should not rise, and I_a is the minimum current, causing operation of the circuit protective device within 5 s.

For example, suppose a 45 A BS 3036 fuse protects a cooker circuit. The disconnection time for the circuit cannot be met, and so a supplementary bonding conductor has been installed between the cooker case and the adjacent metal sink. The resistance R of that conductor should not be greater than $50/I_a$, which in this case is 145 A (IEE Regulations). So:

$$50/145 = 0.34 \; \Omega$$

How, then, do we conduct a test to establish continuity of main or supplementary bonding conductors? Quite simple really: just connect the leads from the continuity tester to the ends of the bonding conductor (Figure 6.1). One end should be disconnected from its bonding clamp, otherwise any measurement may include the resistance of parallel paths of other earthed metalwork. Remember to zero or null the instrument first or, if this facility is not available, record the resistance of the test leads so that this value can be subtracted from the test reading.

Important Note

If the installation is in operation, then never disconnect main bonding conductors unless the supply can be isolated. Without isolation, persons and livestock are at risk of electric shock.

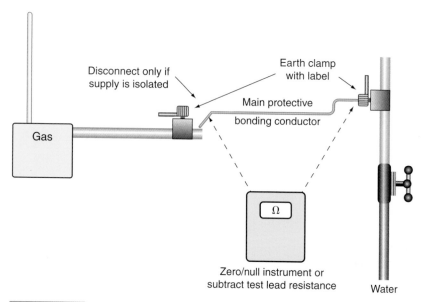

FIGURE 6.1 Continuity of main protective bonding conductor.

The continuity of circuit protective conductors may be established in the same way, but a second method is preferred, as the results of this second test indicate the value of $(R_1 + R_2)$ for the circuit in question.

The test is conducted in the following manner:

1. Temporarily link together the line conductor and cpc of the circuit concerned in the distribution board or consumer unit.
2. Test between line and cpc at each outlet in the circuit. A reading indicates continuity.
3. Record the test result obtained at the furthest point in the circuit. This value is $(R_1 + R_2)$ for the circuit.

Figure 6.2 illustrates the above method.

There may be some difficulty in determining the $(R_1 + R_2)$ values of circuits in installations that comprise steel conduit and trunking, and/or SWA and mims cables because of the parallel earth paths

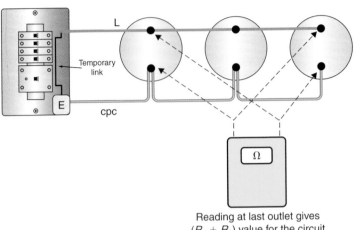

Reading at last outlet gives
$(R_1 + R_2)$ value for the circuit

FIGURE 6.2 CPC continuity.

that are likely to exist. In these cases, continuity tests may have to be carried out at the installation stage before accessories are connected or terminations made off as well as after completion.

Continuity of ring final circuit conductors

There are two main reasons for conducting this test:

1. To establish that interconnections in the ring do not exist.
2. To ensure that the circuit conductors are continuous, and indicate the value of $(R_1 + R_2)$ for the ring.

What then are interconnections in a ring circuit, and why is it important to locate them? Figure 6.3 shows a ring final circuit with an interconnection.

The most likely cause of the situation shown in Figure 6.3 is where a DIY enthusiast has added sockets P, Q, R and S to an existing ring A, B, C, D, E and F. In itself there is nothing wrong

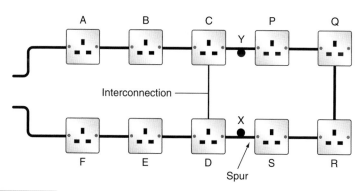

FIGURE 6.3 Ring circuit with interconnection.

with this. The problem arises if a break occurs at, say, point Y, or the terminations fail in socket C or P. Then there would be four sockets all fed from the point X which would then become a spur. So, how do we identify such a situation with or without breaks at point Y? A simple resistance test between the ends of the line, neutral or circuit protective conductors will only indicate that a circuit exists, whether there are interconnections or not. The following test method is based on the theory that the resistance measured across any diameter of a perfect circle of conductor will always be the same value (Figure 6.4).

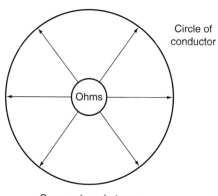

FIGURE 6.4

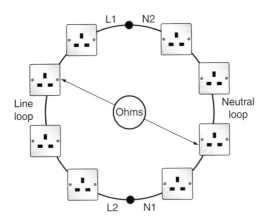

FIGURE 6.5   Circle formed by cross connection.

The perfect circle of conductor is achieved by cross-connecting the line and neutral loops of the ring (Figure 6.5).

The test procedure is as follows:

1. *Identify the opposite legs of the ring.* This is quite easy with sheathed cables, but with singles, each conductor will have to be identified, probably by taking resistance measurements between each one and the closest socket outlet. This will give three high readings and three low readings, thus establishing the opposite legs.
2. *Take a resistance measurement between the ends of each conductor loop. Record this value.*
3. *Cross-connect the ends of the line and neutral loops* (see Figure 6.6).
4. *Measure between line and neutral at each socket on the ring.* The readings obtained should be, for a perfect ring, substantially the same.

If an interconnection existed such as shown in Figure 6.3 then sockets A to F would all have similar readings, and those beyond

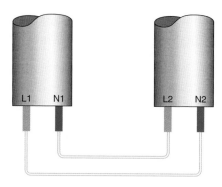

FIGURE 6.6   L and N cross connection.

the interconnection would have gradually increasing values to approximately the midpoint of the ring, then decreasing values back towards the interconnection. If a break had occurred at point Y then the readings from socket S would increase to a maximum at socket P. One or two high readings are likely to indicate either loose connections or spurs. A null reading, i.e. an open circuit indication, is probably a reverse polarity, either line-cpc or neutral-cpc reversal. These faults would clearly be rectified and the test at the suspect socket(s) repeated.

5. *Repeat the above procedure, but in this case cross-connect the line and cpc loops.* In this instance, if the cable is of the flat twin type, the readings at each socket will very slightly increase and then decrease around the ring. This difference, due to the line and cpc being different sizes, will not be significant enough to cause any concern. The measured value is very important it is $(R_1 + R_2)$ for the ring.

As before, loose connections, spurs and, in this case, L–N cross-polarity will be picked up.

The details that follow are typical approximate ohmic values for a healthy 70 m ring final circuit wired in 2.5 mm²/1.5 mm² flat twin and cpc cable:

	L1–L2	N1–N2	cpc1–cpc2
Initial measurements			
Reading at each socket	0.26 Ω	0.26 Ω	between 0.32 Ω and 0.34 Ω
For spurs, each metre in length will add the following resistance to the above values	0.015 Ω	0.015 Ω	0.02 Ω

Insulation resistance

This is probably the most used and yet most abused test of them all. Affectionately known as 'meggering', an insulation resistance test is performed in order to ensure that the insulation of conductors, accessories and equipment is in a healthy condition, and will prevent dangerous leakage currents between conductors and between conductors and earth. It also indicates whether any short circuits exist.

Insulation resistance is the resistance measured between conductors and is made up of countless millions of resistances in parallel (Figure 6.7).

The more resistances there are in parallel, the lower the overall resistance, and in consequence, the longer a cable the lower the insulation resistance. Add to this the fact that almost all installation circuits are also wired in parallel, and it becomes apparent that tests on large installations may give, if measured as a whole, pessimistically low values, even if there are no faults. Under these circumstances, it is usual to break down such large installations into smaller sections, floor by floor, distribution circuit by distribution circuit, etc. This also helps, in the case of periodic testing, to minimize disruption.

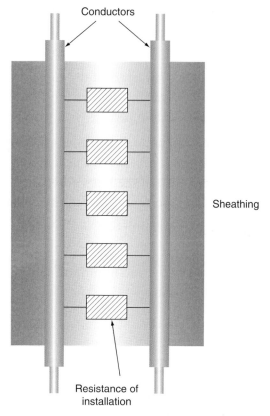

Conductors

Sheathing

Resistance of
installation

FIGURE 6.7   Cable insulation resistance.

The test procedure, then, is as follows:

1. Disconnect all items of equipment such as capacitors
   and indicator lamps as these are likely to give misleading
   results. Remove any items of equipment likely to be
   damaged by the test, such as dimmer switches, electronic
   timers, etc. Remove all lamps and accessories and
   disconnect fluorescent and discharge fittings. Ensure that
   the installation is disconnected from the supply, all fuses
   are in place, and CBs and switches are in the on position.

In some instances it may be impracticable to remove lamps, etc. and in this case the local switch controlling such equipment may be left in the off position.

2. Join together all live conductors of the supply and test between this join and earth. Alternatively, test between each live conductor and earth in turn.

3. Test between line and neutral. For three-phase systems, join together all lines and test between this join and neutral. Then test between each of the lines. Alternatively, test between each of the live conductors in turn. Installations incorporating two-way lighting systems should be tested twice with the two-way switches in alternative positions.

Table 6.2 gives the test voltages and minimum values of insulation resistance for ELV and LV systems.

Table 6.2

System	Test Voltage	Minimum Insulation Resistance
SELV and PELV	250 V DC	0.5 MΩ
LV up to 500 V	500 V DC	1.0 MΩ
Over 500 V	1000 V DC	1.0 MΩ

If a value of less than $2\,M\Omega$ is recorded it may indicate a situation where a fault is developing, but as yet still complies with the minimum permissible value. In this case each circuit should be tested separately to identify any that are suspect.

Polarity

This simple test, often overlooked, is just as important as all the others, and many serious injuries and electrocutions could have been prevented if only polarity checks had been carried out.

The requirements are:

- all fuses and single pole switches are in the line conductor
- the centre contact of an Edison screw type lampholder is connected to the line conductor
- all socket outlets and similar accessories are correctly wired.

Although polarity is towards the end of the recommended test sequence, it would seem sensible, on lighting circuits for example, to conduct this test at the same time as that for continuity of cpcs (Figure 6.8).

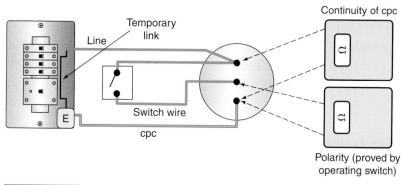

FIGURE 6.8   Lighting polarity.

As discussed earlier, polarity on ring final circuit conductors is achieved simply by conducting the ring circuit test. For radial socket outlet circuits, however, this is a little more difficult. The continuity of the cpc will have already been proved by linking line and cpc and measuring between the same terminals at each socket. Whilst a line-cpc reversal would not have shown, a line-neutral reversal would, as there would have been no reading registered at the socket in question. This would have been remedied, and so only line-cpc reversals need to be checked. This can be done by linking together line and neutral at the origin and testing between the same terminals at each socket. A line-CPC reversal will result in no reading at the socket in question.

Earth electrode resistance

As we know, in many rural areas, the supply system is TT and hence reliance is placed on the general mass of earth for a return path under earth fault conditions and the connection to earth is made by an electrode, usually of the rod type.

In order to determine the resistance of the earth return path, it is necessary to measure the resistance that the electrode has with earth. In this instance an earth fault loop impedance test is carried out between the incoming line terminal and the electrode (a standard test for Z_e). The value obtained is added to the cpc resistance of the protected circuits and this value is multiplied by the operating current of the RCD. The resulting value should not exceed 50 V.

Earth fault loop impedance

Overcurrent protective devices must, under earth fault conditions, disconnect fast enough to reduce the risk of electric shock. This is achieved if the actual value of the earth fault loop impedance does not exceed the tabulated maximum values given in BS 7671. The purpose of the test, therefore, is to determine the actual value of the loop impedance Z_s, for comparison with those maximum values, and it is conducted as follows:

1. Ensure that all main protective bonding is in place.
2. Connect the test instrument either by its BS 1363 plug, or the 'flying leads', to the line, neutral and earth terminals at the remote end of the circuit under test. (If a neutral is not available, connect the neutral probe to earth.)
3. Press to test and record the value indicated.

Table 6.3 Values of Loop Impedance for Comparison with Test Readings.

Protection	Disconnection Time		5 A	6 A	10 A	15 A	16 A	20 A	25 A	30 A	32 A	40 A	45 A	50 A	60 A	63 A	80 A	100 A	125 A	160 A
BS 3036 fuse	0.4 s	Z_s max	7.6	—	—	2.04	—	1.41	—	0.87	—	—	—	—	—	—	—	—	—	—
	5 s	Z_s max	14.16	—	—	4.2	—	3.06	—	2.11	—	—	1.27	—	0.89	—	—	0.42	—	—
BS 88 fuse	0.4 s	Z_s max	—	6.82	4.09	—	2.16	1.42	1.15	—	0.83	—	—	—	—	—	—	—	—	—
	5 s	Z_s max	—	10.8	5.94	—	3.33	2.32	1.84	—	1.47	1.08	—	0.83	—	0.67	0.45	0.33	0.26	0.2
BS 1361 fuse	0.4 s	Z_s max	8.36	—	—	2.62	—	1.36	—	0.92	—	—	—	—	—	—	—	—	—	—
	5 s	Z_s max	13.12	—	—	4	—	2.24	—	1.47	—	—	0.79	—	0.56	—	0.4	0.29	—	—
BS 1362 fuses	0.4 s	Z_s max	(3A) 13.12			(13A) 1.9	—	—	—	—	—	—	—	—	—	—	—	—	—	—
	5 s	Z_s max	(3A) 18.56			(13A) 3.06	—	—	—	—	—	—	—	—	—	—	—	—	—	—
BS 3871 MCB Type 1	0.4 & 5 s	Z_s max	9.2	7.6	4.6	3.06	2.87	2.3	1.84	1.53	1.44	1.15	1.02	0.92	—	0.73	—	—	—	—
BS 3871 MCB Type 2	0.4 & 5 s	Z_s max	5.25	4.37	2.62	1.75	1.64	1.31	1.05	0.87	0.82	0.67	0.58	0.52	—	0.42	—	—	—	—
BS 3871 MCB Type 3	0.4 & 5 s	Z_s max	3.68	3	1.84	1.22	1.15	0.92	0.74	0.61	0.57	0.46	0.41	0.37	—	0.29	—	—	—	—
BS EN 60898 CB Type B	0.4 & 5 s	Z_s max	(3A) 12.26	6.13	3.68	—	2.3	1.84	1.47	—	1.15	0.92	—	0.74	—	0.58	0.46	0.37	0.3	—
BS EN 60898 CB Type C	0.4 & 5 s	Z_s max	—	3.06	1.84	—	1.15	0.92	0.75	—	0.57	0.46	—	0.37	—	0.288	0.23	0.18	0.15	—
BS EN 60898 CB Type D	0.4 & 5 s	Z_s max	1.54	0.92	—	—	0.57	0.46	0.37	—	0.288	0.23	—	0.18	—	0.14	0.12	0.09	0.07	—

It must be understood that this instrument reading is *not valid for direct comparison with the tabulated maximum values*, as account must be taken of the ambient temperature at the time of test, and the maximum conductor operating temperature, both of which will have an effect on conductor resistance. Hence, the $(R_1 + R_2)$ is likely to be greater at the time of fault than at the time of test.

So, our measured value of Z_s must be corrected using correction factors and applying them in a formula.

Clearly this method of correcting Z_s is time-consuming and unlikely to be commonly used. Hence, a rule of thumb method may be applied which simply requires that the measured value of Z_s does not exceed 0.8 of the appropriate tabulated value. Table 6.3 gives the 0.8 values of tabulated loop impedance for direct comparison with measured values.

In effect, a loop impedance test places a line/earth fault on the installation, and if an RCD is present it may not be possible to conduct the test, as the device will trip out each time the loop impedance tester button is pressed. Unless the instrument is of a type that has a built-in guard against such tripping, the value of Z_s will have to be determined from measured values of Z_e and $(R_1 + R_2)$.

Important Note

Never short out an an RCD in order to conduct this test.

As a loop impedance test creates a high earth fault current, albeit for a short space of time, some lower rated CBs may operate, resulting in the same situation as with an RCD, and Z_s will have to be calculated. It is not really good practice to temporarily replace the CB with one of a higher rating.

External loop impedance Z_e

The value of Z_e is measured at the intake position on the supply side and with all main protective bonding disconnected. Unless the installation can be isolated from the supply, this test should not be carried out, as a potential shock risk will exist with the supply on and the main protective bonding disconnected.

Additional protection RCD/RCBO operation

Where RCDs/RCBOs are fitted, it is essential that they operate within set parameters. The RCD testers used are designed to do just this, and the basic tests required are as follows:

1. Set the test instrument to the rating of the RCD.
2. Set the test instrument to half-rated trip.
3. Operate the instrument and the RCD should not trip.
4. Set the instrument to deliver the full rated tripping current of the RCD, $I_{\Delta n}$.
5. Operate the instrument and the RCD should trip out in the required time.
6. For RCDs rated at 30 mA or less set the instrument to deliver 5 times the rated tripping current of the RCD, $5I_{\Delta n}$.
7. Operate the instrument and the RCD should trip out in 40 ms.

Table 6.4 gives further details.

Prospective fault current

Prospective fault current (PFC) has to be determined at the origin of the installation. This is achieved by enquiry, calculation or measurement.

Table 6.4

RCD Type	Half Rated	Full Trip Current
BS 4293 sockets	no trip	less than 200 ms
BS 4293 with time delay	no trip	½ time delay + 200 ms
BS EN 61009 or BS EN 61009 RCBO	no trip	300 ms
As above, but type S with time delay	no trip	130–500 ms

Check of phase sequence

Where multi-phase systems are used there is a high possibility that phase sequence will need to be checked.

This is done with the use of a phase rotation indicator, which, simplistically, is a small three-phase motor.

Functional testing

All RCDs have a built-in test facility in the form of a test button. Operating this test facility creates an artificial out-of-balance condition that causes the device to trip. This only checks the mechanics of the tripping operation; it is not a substitute for the tests just discussed.

All other items of equipment such as switchgear, control gear, interlocks, etc. must be checked to ensure that they are correctly mounted and adjusted and that they function correctly.

Verification of voltage drop

Where required the voltage drop to the furthest point of a circuit should be determined. This is not usually needed for initial verification.

CHAPTER 7

Special Locations
IEE Regulations Part 7

INTRODUCTION

The bulk of BS 7671 relates to typical, single- and three-phase, installations. There are, however, some special installations or locations that have particular requirements. Such locations may present the user/occupant with an increased risk of death or injuries from electric shock.

BS 7671 categorizes these special locations in Part 7 and they comprise the following:

Section 701	Bathrooms, shower rooms, etc.
Section 702	Swimming pools and other basins
Section 703	Rooms containing sauna heaters
Section 704	Construction and demolition sites
Section 705	Agricultural and horticultural premises
Section 706	Conducting locations with restrictive movement
Section 708	Caravan/camping parks
Section 709	Marinas and similar locations
Section 711	Exhibitions shows and stands
Section 712	Solar photovoltaic (PV) power supply systems
Section 717	Mobile or transportable units
Section 721	Caravans and motor caravans
Section 740	Amusement devices, fairgrounds, circuses, etc.
Section 753	Floor and ceiling heating systems

Let us now briefly investigate the main requirements for each of these special locations.

BS 7671 SECTION 701: BATHROOMS, ETC.

This section deals with rooms containing baths, shower basins or areas where showers exist but with tiled floors, for example leisure/recreational centres, sports complexes, etc.

Each of these locations are divided into zones 0, 1 and 2, which give an indication of their extent and the equipment/wiring, etc. that can be installed in order to reduce the risk of electric shock.

So! Out with the tape measure, only to find that in a one-bedroom flat, there may be no zone 2. How can you conform to BS 7671?

The stark answer (mine) is that you may not be able to conform exactly. You do the very best you can in each particular circumstance to ensure safety. Let us not forget that the requirements of BS 7671 are based on reasonableness.

Zone 0

This is the interior of the bath tub or shower basin or, in the case of a shower area without a tray, it is the space having a depth of 100 mm above the floor out to a radius of 600 mm from a fixed shower head or 1200 mm radius for a demountable head (Figure 7.1).

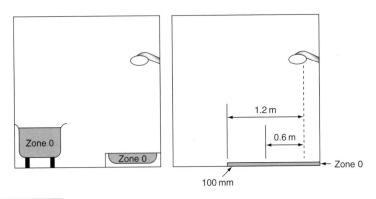

FIGURE 7.1

Zone 1

This extends above zone 0 around the perimeter of the bath or shower basin to 2.25 m above the floor level, and includes any space below the bath or basin that is accessible without the use of a key or tool. For showers without basins, zone 1 extends out to a radius of 600 mm from a fixed shower head or 1200 mm radius for a demountable head (Figure 7.2).

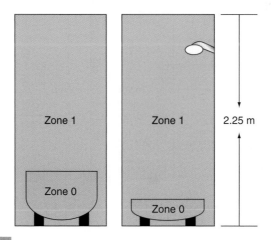

FIGURE 7.2

Note

- Other than switches and controls of equipment specifically designed for use in this zone, and cord operated switches, only SELV switches are permitted.
- Provided they are suitable, fixed items of current using equipment such as:
  Showers
  Shower pumps
  Towell rails
  Luminaires
  Etc.
- Equipment designed for use in this zone must be to at least IPX4, or IPX5, where water jets are likely to be used for cleaning purposes.

Zone 2

This extends 600 mm beyond zone 1 and to a height of 2.25 m above floor level (Figure 7.3).

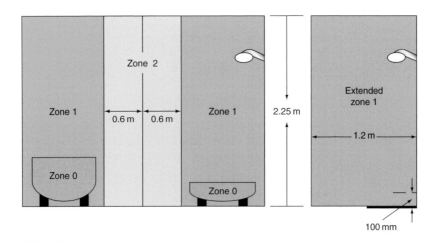

FIGURE 7.3

Note

- Other than switches and controls of equipment specifically designed for use in this zone, and cord operated switches, only SELV switches are permitted.
- Equipment designed for use in this zone must be to at least IPX4, or IPX5 where water jets are likely to be used for cleaning purposes.
- For showers without basins there is no zone 2, just an extended zone 1.
- Socket outlets other than SELV may not be installed within 3 m of the boundary of zone 1.

Supplementary equipotential bonding

Supplementary bonding may be established connecting together the cpcs, exposed and extraneous conductive parts within the location.

Such extraneous conductive parts will include:

- metallic gas, water, waste and central heating pipes
- metallic structural parts that are accessible to touch
- metal baths and shower basins.

This bonding may be carried out inside or outside the location, preferably close to the entry of the extraneous conductive parts to the location.

However, this bonding may be omitted if the premises has a protective earthing and automatic disconnection system in place; all extraneous conductive parts of the locations are connected to the protective bonding and all circuits are residual current device (RCD) protected (which they have to be anyway!!).

Electric floor units may be installed below any zone provided that they are covered with an earthed metal grid or metallic sheath and connected to the protective conductor of the supply circuit.

BS 7671 SECTION 702: SWIMMING POOLS

In a similar fashion to bathrooms and shower rooms, etc., swimming pool locations are also divided into zones 0, 1 and 2:

Zone 0 is in the pool/basin or fountain.

Zone 1 extends 2.0 m horizontally from the rim of zone 0 and 2.5 m vertically above it regardless of the pool being above or below ground level. If there are diving boards, shutes or viewing galleries, etc. the height extends to a point 2.5 m from their top surface and 1.5 m horizontally either side of such shutes, etc.

Zone 2 extends a further 1.5 m horizontally from the edge of zone 1 and 2.5 m above ground level.

Now, what can we install in these zones?

Zones 0 and 1

Protection against shock

Only SELV to be used.

Wiring systems

Only systems supplying equipment in these zones are permitted. Metal cable sheaths or metallic covering of wiring systems shall be connected to the supplementary equipotential bonding. Cables should preferably be enclosed in PVC conduit.

Switchgear, control gear and socket outlets

None permitted except for locations where there is no zone 2. In this case a switch or socket outlet with an insulated cap or cover may be installed beyond 1.25 m from the edge of zone 0 at a height of no less than 300 mm. Additionally, the circuits must be protected by:

1. SELV or
2. Automatic disconnection using a 30 mA RCD or
3. Electrical separation.

Equipment

Only that which is designed for these locations.

Other equipment may be used when the pool/basin is not in use (cleaning, maintenance, etc.) provided the circuits are protected by:

1. SELV or
2. Automatic disconnection using a 30 mA RCD or
3. Electrical separation.

Socket outlets and control devices should have a warning notice indicating to the user that they should not be used unless the location is unoccupied by persons.

Zone 2 (there is no zone 2 for fountains)

Switchgear and control gear

Socket outlets and switches, provided they are protected by:

1. SELV or
2. Automatic disconnection using a 30 mA RCD or
3. Electrical separation.

IP rating of enclosures

Zone 0 IPX8 (submersion)
Zone 1 IPX4 (splashproof) or IPX5 (where water jets are used for cleaning)

Zone 2 IPX2 (drip proof) indoor pools
IPX4 (splashproof) outdoor pools
IPX5 (where water jets are used for cleaning).

Supplementary bonding

All extraneous conductive parts in zones 0, 1 and 2 must be connected by supplementary bonding conductors to the protective conductors of exposed conductive parts in these zones.

BS 7671 SECTION 703: HOT AIR SAUNAS

Once again a zonal system, that is, 1, 2 and 3, has been used as per Figure 7.4. In this case the zones are based on temperature.

Sauna room

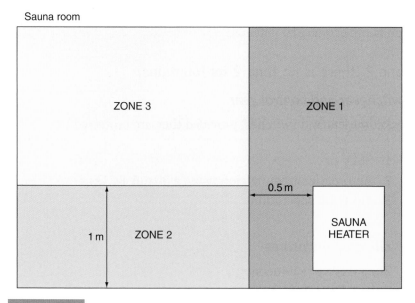

FIGURE 7.4

Additional protection

All circuits in the location should have additional protection against shock by 30 mA RCDs except sauna heater circuits unless recommended by the manufacturer.

Wiring systems

It is preferred that the wiring systems for the sauna will be installed outside. However, any wiring inside should be heat resisting and any metal sheaths or conduit must be inaccessible in normal use.

Equipment

All should be at least IPX4 and IPX5 if water jets are to be used for cleaning:

Zone 1 only the sauna equipment
Zone 2 no restriction regarding temperature resistance
Zone 3 must be suitable for 125°C and cable sheaths for 175°C.

Switchgear, control gear and accessories

Only that which is associated with the sauna heater equipment may be installed in zone 2 and in accordance with the manufacturer's instructions. All other should be outside.

BS 7671 SECTION 704: CONSTRUCTION SITES

Not as complicated as one may think. The only areas that require special consideration are where construction work is being carried out, not site huts, etc.

So, let us keep all this as simple as possible. Clearly, construction sites are hazardous areas and in consequence the shock risk is greater.

Protection

For socket outlet circuits of rating up to and including 32 A and circuits supplying equipment of rating up to and including 32 A, the means of protection shall be:

1. Reduced low voltage (preferred for portable hand tools and hand lamps up to 2 kW)
2. Automatic disconnection of supply with additional protection by 30 mA RCDs
3. Electrical separation
4. SELV or PELV (SELV being preferred for portable hand lamps in damp locations).

For socket outlet circuits rated above 32 A, a 500 mA RCD is required.

External influences

These are not addressed in BS 7671, presumably as there are so many different possibilities. So common sense must prevail and equipment used with an appropriate degree of protection in accordance with the severity of the influence.

Wiring systems

Apart from some requirements for flexible cables, the only comment relates to ensuring that cables that pass under site roads, etc. are protected against mechanical damage.

Isolation and switching

An Assembly for Construction Sites (ACS), which is basically the main intake supply board, should comprise a lockable isolator and, for current using equipment and socket outlets:

1. Overcurrent devices
2. Fault protective devices
3. Socket outlets if required.

Plugs and sockets/cable couplers

All should be to BS EN 60309-2.

BS 7671 SECTION 705: AGRICULTURAL AND HORTICULTURAL LOCATIONS

The requirements apply only to locations that do not include the main farmhouse outside of which the environment is hazardous and where, of course, livestock is present (animals are susceptible to lethal shock levels at 25 V AC).

Protection

Protection against shock may be provided by:

1. Automatic disconnection of supply with additional RCD protection for:
   (a) Final circuits supplying socket outlets rated at 32 A or less (30 mA)
   (b) Final circuits supplying socket outlets rated more than 32 A (100 mA)
   (c) All other circuits (300 mA).
2. SELV or PELV.

Protection against thermal effects:

1. Heating appliances should be mounted at appropriate distances from combustible materials and livestock, with radiant heaters at a minimum distance of 0.5 m.
2. For fire protection an RCD rated at 300 mA or less should be used.

Supplementary bonding

Wherever livestock is housed, supplementary bonding must be carried out connecting all exposed and extraneous conductive parts that can be touched by livestock. All metal grids in floors must be connected to the supplementary equipotential bonding.

External influences

1. All equipment must be to at least IP44 and luminaires exposed to dust and moisture ingress, IP54.
2. Appropriate protection for socket outlets where influences are greater than AD4, AE3 and/or AG1.
3. Appropriate protection where corrosive substances are present.

Diagrams

The user of the installation should be provided with plans and diagrams showing the location of all equipment, concealed cable routes, distribution and the equipotential bonding system.

Wiring systems

Any, just as long as it is suitable for the environment and fulfils the required minimum degrees of protection.

A high impact PVC conduit/trunking system would be appropriate in many cases as it is not affected by corrosion, is rodent proof and has no exposed conductive parts. However, the system would be designed to suit the particular environmental conditions.

Wiring systems should be erected so as to be, where possible, inaccessible to livestock. Overhead lines should be insulated and, where vehicles/mobile equipment are used, underground cables should be at least 0.6 m deep and mechanically protected and 1.0 m deep in arable land.

Self-supporting suspended cables should be at a height of at least 6 m.

Switchgear and control gear

Whatever! As long as it is suitable for the conditions and that emergency switching is placed in a position inaccessible to livestock and can be accessed in the event of livestock panic (Stampede!!!).

BS 7671 SECTION 706: RESTRICTIVE CONDUCTIVE LOCATIONS

These are very rare locations which could include metal tanks, boilers, ventilation ducts, etc., where access is required for maintenance, repair or inspection. Bodily movement will be severely restricted and in consequence such areas are extremely dangerous.

This section deals with the installation inside the location and the requirements for bringing in accessories/equipment from outside.

For fixed equipment in the location, one of the following methods of protection shall be used:

1. Automatic disconnection of supply but with additional supplementary bonding
2. The use of Class II equipment backed up by a 30 mA RCD
3. Electrical separation
4. SELV.

For hand-held lamps and tools and mobile equipment, SELV or electrical separation should be used.

BS 7671 SECTION 708: CARAVAN AND CAMPING PARKS

We drive into a caravan/camping park for our holiday and need to connect to a supply of electricity for all our usual needs. This is accommodated by the provision of suitably placed socket outlets, supplied via distribution circuits.

External influences

Equipment should have at least the following protection codes:

1. IPX4 for the presence of splashes (AD4)
2. IP3X for presence of small objects (AE2)
3. IK08 for presence of high severity mechanical stress (AG3) (the IK codes are for impact and 08 is an impact of 5 joules).

Wiring systems

The distribution circuits are erected either underground or overhead:

1. Underground cable (preferred) should be suitably protected against mechanical damage, tent pegs, steel spikes, etc. and at a depth of no less than 0.6 m.
2. If overhead, then 6 m above ground where there is vehicle movement and 3.5 m elsewhere.

Switchgear and socket outlets

1. Supply equipment should be adjacent to, or within 20 m of, the pitch.

2. Socket outlets should be: to BS EN 60309-2; IP44, at between 0.5 m and 1.5 m above ground, rated not less than 16 A and have individual overcurrent and 30 mA RCD protection.

3. If the supply is TN-C-S the protective conductor of each socket needs to be connected to an earth rod.

BS 7671 SECTION 709: MARINAS

This location is basically a camping park for boats and has similar requirements to those of caravan/camping parks.

It is where you arrive in your 40 ft 8 berth cruiser (some hope) looking for a place to park!!!

However, the environment is a little more harsh than the caravan park due to the possibilities of corrosion, mechanical damage, structural movement and flammable fuels, together with the increased risk of electric shock.

External influences

Due to the harsh conditions mentioned the classification of influences would include:

AD water
AE solid foreign bodies
AF corrosion and
AG impact.

Wiring systems

Distribution circuits, like those in caravan parks, can be either underground or overhead, as well as PVC covered mineral insulated, cables in cable management systems, etc.

However, overhead cables on or incorporating a support wire, cables with aluminium conductors or mineral insulated cables shall not be installed above a jetty or pontoon, etc.

Underground cables should have additional mechanical protection and be installed 0.5 m deep.

Overhead cables should be at the same heights as in caravan parks.

Isolation, switching and socket outlets

Generally the same as caravan parks.

Socket outlets should be installed not less than 1 m above the highest water level except that for floating pontoons, walkways, etc. this height may be reduced to 300 mm.

BS 7671 SECTION 711: EXHIBITIONS, SHOWS AND STANDS

This section deals with the protection of the users of temporary structures erected in or out of doors and is typical of antique fairs, motorbike shows, arts and craft exhibitions, etc.

It does not cover public or private events that form part of entertainment activities, which are the subject of BS 7909.

External influences

None particularly specified. Clearly they must be considered and addressed accordingly.

Wiring

Armoured or mechanically protected cables where there is a risk of mechanical damage.

Cables shall have a minimum conductor size of 1.5 mm^2.

Protection

Against shock:

1. Supply cables to a stand or unit, etc. must be protected at the cable origin by a time-delayed RCD of residual current rating not exceeding 300 mA.
2. All socket outlet circuits not exceeding 32 A and all other final circuits, excepting emergency lighting, shall have additional protection by 30 mA RCDs.
3. Any metallic structural parts accessible from within the unit stand, etc. shall be connected by a main protective bonding conductor to the main earthing terminal of the unit.

Against thermal effects:

1. Clearly in this case all luminaires, spot lights, etc. should be placed in such positions as not to cause a build-up of excessive heat that could result in fire or burns.

Isolation

Every unit, etc. should have a readily accessible and identifiable means of isolation.

Inspection and testing

Tongue in cheek here!! Every installation **should** be inspected and tested on site in accordance with Part 6 of BS 7671.

BS 7671 SECTION 712: SOLAR PHOTOVOLTAIC (PV) SUPPLY SYSTEMS

These are basically solar panels generating DC which is then converted to AC via an invertor. Those dealt with in BS 7671 relate to those systems that are used to 'top up' the normal supply.

There is a need for consideration of the external influences that may affect cabling from the solar units outside to control gear inside.

There must be protection against overcurrent and a provision made for isolation on both the DC and AC sides of the invertor.

As the systems can be used in parallel with or as a switched alternative to the public supply, reference should be made to Chapter 55 of BS 7671.

BS 7671 SECTION 717: MOBILE OR TRANSPORTABLE UNITS

Medical facilities units, mobile workshops, canteens, etc. are the subject of this section. They are self-contained with their own installation and designed to be connected to a supply by, for instance, a plug and socket.

The standard installation protective measures against shock are required with the added requirement that the automatic disconnection of the supply should be by means of an RCD.

Also all socket outlets for the use of equipment outside the unit should have additional protection by 30 mA RCDs.

The supply cable should be HO7RN-F, oil and flame resistant heavy duty rubber with a minimum copper conductor size of 2.5 mm^2.

Socket outlets outside should be to a minimum of IP44.

BS 7671 SECTION 721: CARAVANS AND MOTOR CARAVANS

These are the little homes that people tow behind their cars or that are motorized, not those that tend to be located on a fixed site. It would be unusual for the general Electrical Contractor to wire new, or even rewire old units. How many of us ever rewire our cars? In consequence, only the very basic requirements are considered here.

Protection

These units are small houses on wheels and subject to the basic requirements of protection against shock and overcurrent. Where automatic disconnection of supply is used this must be provided by a 30 mA RCD.

Wiring systems

The wiring systems should take into account the fact that the structure of the unit is subject to flexible/mechanical stresses and, therefore, our common flat twin and three-core cables should not be used.

Inlets

Unless the caravan demand exceeds 16 A, the inlet should conform to the following:

(a) To BS EN 60309-1 or 2 if interchangeability is required
(b) No more than 1.8 m above ground level
(c) Readily accessible and in a suitable enclosure outside the caravan
(d) Identified by a notice that details the nominal voltage, frequency and rated current of the unit.

Also, inside the caravan, there should be an isolating switch and a notice detailing the instructions for the connection and disconnection of the electricity supply and the period of time between inspection and testing (3 years).

General

Accessories and luminaires should be arranged such that no damage can occur due to movement, etc.

There should be no compatibility between sockets of low and extra low voltage.

Any accessory exposed to moisture should be IP55 rated (jet proof and dust proof).

BS 7671 SECTION 740: AMUSEMENT DEVICES, FAIRGROUNDS, CIRCUSES, ETC.

This is not an area that is familiar to most installation electricians and hence will only be dealt with very briefly.

The requirements of this section are very similar to those of Section 711 Exhibitions, shows, etc. and parts of Section 706 Agricultural locations (because of animals) regarding supplementary bonding.

For example, additional protection by 30 mA is required for:

1. Lighting circuits, except those that are placed out of arm's reach and not supplied via socket outlets.
2. All socket outlet circuits rated up to 32 A.
3. Mobile equipment supplied by a flexible cable rated up to 32 A.

Automatic disconnection of supply must be by an RCD.

Equipment should be rated to at least IP44.

The installation between the origin and any equipment should be inspected and tested after each assembly on site.

BS 7671 SECTION 753: FLOOR AND CEILING HEATING SYSTEMS

Systems referred to in this section are those used for thermal storage heating or direct heating.

Protection

Against shock:

1. Automatic disconnection of supply with disconnection achieved by 30 mA RCD.
2. Additional protection for Class II equipment by 30 mA RCDs.
3. Heating systems provided without exposed conductive parts shall have a metallic grid of spacing not more than 300 mm installed on site above a floor system or below a ceiling system and connected to the protective conductor of the system.

Against thermal effects:

1. Where skin or footwear may come into contact with floors the temperature shall be limited, for example to 30°C.
2. To protect against overheating of these systems the temperature of any zone should be limited to a maximum of 80°C.

External influences

Minimum of IPX1 for ceilings and IPX7 for floors.

The designer must provide a comprehensive and detailed plan of the installation which should be fixed on or adjacent to the system distribution board.

Appendix 1
Problems

1. What is the resistance of a 10 m length of 6.0 mm² copper line conductor if the associated cpc is 1.5 mm²?

2. What is the length of a 6.0 mm² copper line conductor with a 2.5 mm² cpc if the overall resistance is 0.189 Ω?

3. If the total loop impedance of a circuit under operating conditions is 0.96 Ω and the cable is a 20 m length of 4.0 mm² copper with a 1.5 mm² cpc, what is the external loop impedance?

4. Will there be a shock risk if a double socket outlet, fed by a 23 m length of 2.5 mm² copper conductor with a 1.5 mm² cpc, is protected by a 20 A BS 3036 rewirable fuse and the external loop impedance is measured as 0.5 Ω?

5. A cooker control unit incorporating a socket outlet is protected by a 32 A BS 88 fuse, and wired in 6.0 mm² copper with a 2.5 mm² cpc. The run is some 25 m and the external loop impedance of the TN-S system is not known. Is there a shock risk.

6. *Design problem*: In a factory it is required to install, side by side, two three-phase 400 V direct on-line motors, each rated at 19 A full load current. There is spare capacity in a three-phase distribution fuseboard housing BS 3036 fuses, and the increased load will not affect the existing installation. The cables are to be PVC-insulated singles installed in steel conduit, and a separate

cpc is required. The earthing system is TN-S with a measured external loop impedance of $0.47\,\Omega$, and the length of the cable run is 42 m. The worst conduit section is 7 m long with one bend. The ambient temperature is not expected to exceed 35°C. Determine the minimum sizes of cable.

Appendix 2
Answers to Problems

1. $0.152\,\Omega$
2. $18\,\text{m}$
3. $0.56\,\Omega$
4. No
5. Yes.
6. *Design problem:* For the factory design problem, the values obtained are as follows:

   $I_b = 19\,\text{A}$;
   $I_n = 20\,\text{A}$;
   $C_c = 0.725$;
   $C_a = 0.94$;
   $C_g = 0.8$;
   $I_t = 36.6\,\text{A}$;
   cable size $= 6.0\,\text{mm}^2$;
   cpc size $= 2.5\,\text{mm}^2$;
   $Z_s = 1\,\Omega$;
   $I = 230\,\text{A}$;
   $t = 1\,\text{s}$;
   $k = 115$.

Index

Index